THE CUTTING EDGE

The Martial Art of Business

Dedicated to Magnus and Freja

Bjørn Aris

THE CUTTING EDGE

The Martial Art of Business

Advice concerning the text: J.W. Arends and W. Vreeswijk

Photos: Frits de Boer and Frank Jansen
Cover photos: Mark Horn

CIP details
ISBN: 978 90 819277 5 8
NUR: 808 / 801
Reference: Leadership/Management

Publisher's note. This book was previously released under the title 'De zon komt op in het Oosten'.

Contents

Introduction

We say, to shine one corner of the World – that is enough. Not the whole World. Just make it clear where you are.
SHUNRYU SUZUKI

Ever since the Renaissance we Westerners have, on the whole, limited ourselves to think using reason and the five senses. Reason guides the way that we do things. We assume that we can understand, figure out and solve all the problems that crop up by using our reason. But is that right? Decisions are made before we have come to a rational conclusion and we are only consciously aware of fifteen to twenty information impulses per second, whilst our subconscious receives eleven million impulses per second. Our reason is merely the tip of the iceberg. Is our reason really the thing that is guiding us?

Through being steered purely by our reason and the five senses, we alienate the bigger picture. You see this in people as well as within companies. People often feel isolated or depressed. They get the feeling that they have become something that is just tossed around by (global) forces over which they no longer have control. They miss the connection with other people, with society and with nature. Western companies are increasingly faced with problems that they are unable to resolve themselves, no matter how much they reorganize and no matter how many consultants they use. Managers become estranged from their employees and companies have difficulty introducing new ideas before it's too late.

To solve these problems we have to step outside the traditional frameworks of how we think.

In the East people think in a very different way. In this book you will be introduced to the Japanese solutions to Western problems, also using the Japanese Way of the Sword. This is the Way that the Samurai chose and the Way that their descendants still choose today in their private and work life. This Way begins with Zen and travels via Ki (life force) and Bushido (the Samurai's code of conduct). The Way of the Sword is a metaphor, but is also a source of knowledge and understanding. Companies like Honda and Toyota follow this Way and it has contributed to their success. What can companies in the West learn from Japan in general, from the Way of the Sword and from successful Japanese enterprises? And how can leaders, managers and employees use the Japanese way of thinking in their daily lives?

This book is not a scientific oeuvre. It is more the result of 'cherry picking'. And the intention is to inform the reader, by using metaphors, not only taking the rational route but also via other Ways. It is as much a personal tale as an aid for companies and individuals to conduct business in a healthier and more successful way.

The Problem

History

The Western way of thinking leans heavily on reason, especially in Western science. Man is considered to be the only thinking being and is thereby superior to all other beings. Through regarding reason as man's most important feature, feeling and intuition are left unnoticed in the background. Our way of thinking has brought us a long way. Our fridges, washing machines, drainage systems, waterworks, telephones, computers and hospitals are all perfect examples of this. But, our way of thinking has also brought us so far that we can destroy the earth at the push of a button. If there were a balance between reason, feeling and intuition, these kinds of destructive instruments would not be developed.

Medical science is well advanced. We are able to combat many illnesses and we can keep people alive that only a few years ago any doctor would have given up on. At the same time medical science focuses only on the impairment or illness. Western doctors are perfectly capable of being able to cut away tumours but they don't look at the bigger picture. Why did an illness come about, what emotions play a role in the genesis of an illness, and what influence does the spirit have on keeping a body healthy? By focussing on the illness itself and losing sight of the person as a whole, the patient loses his identity and is reduced to being the object being cut into. Through this attitude, people can become isolated and sink into depression.

The Western way of thinking is based on Greek Reductionism, the division of body and soul, and a deterministic, monotheistic view of the world. The Greeks put man at the centre of everything and through this they broke off a part of the natural link with our surroundings. Really, we aren't set apart from nature, we are a part of nature, we are constantly linked to our surroundings and we are a part of something much bigger. Sometimes we feel nature calling us, so we take a Sunday afternoon stroll through the woods and feel the greatness of all those old trees. Then in the evening we're home again and we put the heating up. Nature is something set apart from us – we're no longer a part of it.

We have reduced the world to nothing more than matter

The division between body and spirit was sublimated in the seventeenth century by René Descartes with his: 'I think therefore I am.' From then on man was reduced to being just a thinking head, separate from his feelings and intuitive powers.

Descartes separated body and spirit so that we could consider reason a reality, whilst reason is still 'only' a language.

We have reduced the world to nothing more than matter. The spirit is pushed back into the 'religious section', separate from life, no longer within us, but outside us. It is clear that by separating the body and the spirit, science that focused on matter was ready for an enormous break-through. This actually came about in a big way, resulting in man being reduced to an economic factor, and respect for the spirit and even for human dignity, are now hard to find.

And ultimately, we are going to consider the world, nature and people as a mechanism that complies with natural laws. We study life and take it to pieces, as if it were a car, and we put it back as we think fit, or as something else.

Because of these notions we have started thinking sequentially. One thing leads on to another, everything has a clear beginning and a clear ending. We can perceive parts (and people!) totally separately from one another and split off from the whole picture. Often, we have lost sight of the whole picture. It is interesting to note here that the natural laws as we know them appear to work differently at quantum level. For example, at quantum level, it is possible for a particle to be in two places at once or that small particles that are thousands of kilometres apart from one another, still stay soundly in contact with one another. There is therefore more between heaven and earth than we can logically reason; luckily, we are able to perceive that afore-mentioned 'more'.

Adverse Factors

Conditioning works by making it seem as if you are looking at reality through rose coloured glasses. We get a distorted image of our surroundings. We think we have the overall picture, but we get hold of the wrong details. We are less efficient than we could have been. Nevertheless, conditioning is important. It lays down the basis for how we should treat one another. It is good to realise that you are conditioned and to get a good insight into how you are conditioned.

Conditioning teaches us that 'external' satisfaction makes us feel good, that feeling good is a material state that logically is something on the outside. Yet, feeling good is a feeling and feelings are on the inside. By breaking through conditioning, you are able to make a choice.

It begins with becoming aware of the fact that a craving for material things is something we learn and it is supported by five thousand advertising messages a day. By consciously breaking through this craving for material things, we break the illusion and the habit that saddles us with too much stress. We literally free ourselves of material things. The good feeling that material things bring will quickly disappear.

Here's an example of collective conditioning: When an English politician has a wife and a mistress on the side, he is scorned. In France, just 32 kilometres across the sea, a politician who keeps four mistresses is made President.

If you are tired, your ego is also tired. We definitely mustn't underestimate this second factor. On the one hand, our ego is the driving force behind our development and our perseverance. On the other hand, our ego is a very restricting factor. It influences our instinct and our perception and thereby gets in the way of an optimal collaboration between the left and right sides of our brain. An example of the way our ego works is when you think that you already know something. You are not open to other opinions, ideas or solutions, but you are certain that your view is the only right and true one and that the world would be a better place if everyone were to embrace your point of view. Whoever can turn off their ego, will literally feel that everything and everyone is linked and that everyone comes from the very same source.

A third adverse factor is fear, an important aspect of our conditioning. Fear lets us follow all sorts of beaten tracks, whereas we should really avoid them. Conditioning through scaremongering starts already with our up-bringing. Our parents constantly point out possible dangers and the consequences of our behaviour. In part this is good, because a child without fear would walk out onto the motorway, out of curiosity. But other types of fear we could miss like a sore head.

We are born with two fears: the fear of death and the fear for noise. We are taught all other fears. The disadvantage of these learned fears is that, through them, we continue to refer to our reason. We think about what can go wrong so we are no longer in the here and now. Fear brings stress with it and so the circle is complete. Stress makes sure that you can't relax so you can't make use of any of your other five senses.

Effects on work life

Present in body alone.

People appear to be present at work in body alone, what you may call 'barely with us' or 'on another planet' and even seem anxious. That is because of conditioning. People learn things from all kinds of sources so they no longer have to think for themselves. Through this and thanks to the huge amount of external impulses they are exposed to, people live constantly in a delusional state and no longer in the here and now; they drift.

Overtired

As a result of the fact that they are not living in the here and now and as a result of stress, people become overtired. They have even forgotten what it is like to feel good.

Not a lot of bonding between colleagues

The bonding between colleagues in a company is weak, partially as a result of digitalisation. Work is seen as a means to achieve something, such as happiness, that is seen in our society as a material state that lies outside of us. The bonding amongst colleagues is weak as a result of pressure put on them, and digitalisation.

People sit in traffic for two hours to get to work and sit in their little corner where they send an e-mail to a colleague three doors further up the corridor. The contact with society and the company has also disappeared. A lovely example is the mission statement that became so important around the turn of the century. Every self respecting company hired an advertising company and were handed over a mission statement. This mission statement didn't come from within the company, it was thought up by some external bureau to impress the outside world with beautiful words. Mission statements that are not 'felt' and actually lived out by a company, mean nothing. You won't find a company with a mission statement claiming that they trade in weapons, women or drugs. All mission statements carry the message that the company thinks and works with the interest of society and their customer in mind. But often they are just empty phrases that appear in a glossy Annual Report. The mission statement is not rooted into the company, no policies are raised from it and employees and customers have no way of verifying it. In this way the question: 'What is the purpose of your company on this Earth?' is avoided. No-one really knows what is important and everybody just does something. Through a lack of vision and leadership you create companies with no raison d'être and no direction. As an employee, how then can you possibly get job satisfaction? Managers and leaders that are largely busy with their own career and keeping track of holidays, are not really leaders.

Departments work on islands

Uncoordinated reorganisations will never be successful. One of the complaints often heard about large companies is that the various departments each work on their own little island. They are then told from up above (top-down) how those little islands are going to work together better. In this way, the system is the starting point and not the people on the work floor who actually have to do the work. Of course it is important to develop a vision and a strategy but if the people are not attached to that vision, then the whole project will not work. Colleagues sometimes work with one another for years without knowing anything about each other. How can you expect different departments to work better together when they don't even know one another? The person who takes just an hour out on a Monday morning to discuss the previous week (business) and last weekend (private) with their employees will quickly bear the fruit from it. That little hour is often seen as non-productive and therefore a waste of time. But that little hour does make sure your employees are more motivated. A guaranteed profit!

The result is what counts

Everything is focussed on the result. The results come foremost (quarterly report) and are even forecast. All companies work with forecasts. Without forecasts no business would be done, no credit would be given. But very often forecasts are not complete. Many times they are compiled based on the understanding of well meaning staff, without taking the customer and other deciding factors into account, for example. In this way there is no room given for development, neither for processes, nor people. Please note: development means to unwrap something. So take the wrapping off.

Potential is not used to the full

Companies exist thanks to people (employees and customers). Creativity, the ability to solve problems and job expertise are in abundance in every company, but usually they aren't used to their full potential. Employees can find solutions to problems themselves but, because of the top down way of thinking and the chosen management style, employees are not taken seriously, or even not heard. And those who are excluded, don't feel a bond with the company, will never feel comfortable in his own workplace and will never do more than what appears in his job description.

The more you earn, the happier you are.
The salary that people receive is very different to what people 'earn'. In the West, salary is seen as a performance factor, as if happiness is something external. Happiness is mainly measured by the amount on someone's bank account.

Stress
Employees are exposed to a lot of stress. Someone today receives more information impulses in one day that someone a hundred years ago received in a lifetime.

Lack of trust.
When things are not going well within a company, new people are brought in. Through this, knowledge and experience are lost. This is just contesting the symptoms and it doesn't solve the problem. In some companies there is a constant series of one reorganisation after the other. Expensive consultants are brought in to solve the problems. The message this brings across to their own employees is really: We haven't got the least bit of faith in your being able to do a good job.

Age
Employees older than 35 are, in effect, written off.

A lack of leaders.
Managers can no longer lead. A leader has an overall view, has a long term strategy, he / she is focussed on continuity and he / she knows what the added value of their company is for their customers, employees and society. A leader inspires, provokes and takes overall responsibility. Managers avoid risks, are focussed on short term solutions only for the part that they are responsible for.

Good employees leave

Good employees leave. You find intelligent people up as far as middle management, but in order to reach the top you have to use your elbows and a lot of people don't want to do that.

Organisations are organised top-down.

Western companies have a strong top-down organisation. They are inflexible because too many decisions have to be made by top management, even about things that top management know nothing about. Because of this top-down structure, employees daren't take on responsibility or make decisions. They always address their superiors so the work doesn't get done and companies become bureaucratic.

Crisis brings chances

A crisis is needed for a Western company to be renewed. There are plenty of examples. Banks and insurance companies have been criticised for decades, for example. Consumers have had little faith in them for many years. Yet a financial crisis was needed before an actual change was brought about. The banks have committed to a code of conduct and insurance companies in the Netherlands have joined a programme called Renewed Insurers. Of course this could have a good influence but in the end the change has been set down by society and it doesn't come from inside the company itself. It can be doubted whether or not this is a lucrative basis for innovation.

Who can damage us?

Everything is looked at legally. Through a fear of reputational damage or fines from the authorities, new products or services are not judged by their added value for the customer, but on the basis of compliance: Who can damage us?

Worth and economy

A company's worth has nothing to do with reality. The world of money has, in any case, lost touch with the real economy. Some 95% of world trade is volatile, only 5% is based on real money. We live and work in a worldwide casino with no link to reality. Multinationals have declined into little games for shareholders and hedge fund managers.

Customers are annoying

The customer is a necessary evil. The writing is on the wall when a country such as the Netherlands has a bestseller with the title "*Fucking customers.*"

Development is not implemented

Development takes place mainly within projects (with a clear beginning and a clear end) and it is not continuous. The results of a project are given in a report that later disappears into a drawer somewhere. Then a new project is started. In effect, not a lot changes.

Not enough CSR

Companies have no respect for nature. A lot of financial institutions employ, for example, a lovely CSR programme (Corporate Social Responsibility), but then invest in non-sustainable companies. The consequences of this include: deforestation, pollution and climate change.

These short summaries describe only a few of the problems that companies in the West have to face. You could fill whole books with examples of what is wrong in the business world, and these kinds of books have been written, and more will follow. It's a good thing that these books exist as real change can only take place once it is realized that things really have got to be done differently. Once that realization is there, the crucial question is of course: So how do we do that then? I will strive to answer that question in the following chapters.

Japan has the knowledge that the West lacks. What can we learn from Japan? How can we organise our companies better? And how can we apply their concepts in our daily life?

What Western companies can learn from Japan

The Toyota Way

In *The Toyota Way: 14 Management Principles from the World's Greatest Manufacturer,* J.K. Liker describes Toyota's 14 principles:

Long term vision

1. Have a long term vision, even if this costs you money in the shortterm. For example: in twenty years this company still has to exist to make products that please our customers, provide a home for its employees and to have a function within society.

The right process will deliver the right results

2. Make sure that problems quickly come to light, give them plenty of attention and try not to avoid the issue.

3. Let demand drive production to avoid overproduction; having contact with and knowing your customer is essential for this.

4. Determine production levels very precisely and avoid waste. This is a continual process that should constantly be revised and can always be improved.
5. Make sure that you have a culture in which the production process can be stopped immediately if problems arise so that the product is good from start to finish. With this kind of approach you need to have the involvement of all employees, a strong group feeling and don't point out the person to blame if a mistake is made.
6. Standardised tasks and processes form the basis for continuous improvement and growth within your workforce. This is 'kata' or form (more about this later in the book).
7. Make sure you have visual control so that no problems remain hidden. A pile of paper will wait patiently on your desk. Make sure you can see the problem yourself.
8. Only use reliable, well tested technology that helps people and production.

Add value to the organisation by giving people the chance to develop

9. Train leaders that understand the process, carry out the company's vision and can teach it to others. This means that they don't have any product knowledge; that's what their staff is for.
10. Make sure you have good people and teams that carry out the company's vision. It is very important to invest in personnel and to develop and carry out a joint vision.
11. Respect your network of partners and suppliers by encouraging them to improve and by helping them.

The organisation learns by continuously solving problems

12. Size up the situation yourself to fathom things out. Once there was written: never trust anyone! This means: don't suppose that someone else will do something the same way that you would. Also, by taking a look yourself, you strengthen your link with the work floor and you get an insight into what is really going on there.
13. Make decisions together and make sure there is a consensus, consider all possibilities well and apply the chosen decision quickly. The emphasis is on good preparation: the right process will deliver the right results. If you have got that right, the results will follow and you can implement things quickly. Also, of course, due to the fact that everyone was involved in the process.
14. Be a living organisation by constantly and carefully following and improving work processes. This can only happen if there is good communication and you are all striving for the same goal. And that is also, of course, another continuous process.

It is interesting that we Westerners can understand this rationally but not instinctively. Both leaders and their staff will have to develop individually before the company is able to take on another approach.

That is why in Japan you see that once you turn 35 you are not replaceable, unlike here. The older you get, the more valuable you are thanks to your experience, development and insight.

The Kaizen principle

Toyota works using the Kaizen principle. Kaizen stands for continual improvement and respect for people. The literal meaning of Kaizen is: to take something apart and to build it again in a better way. At Toyota, employees are constantly busy improving their processes, services and products. This is why the company is so successful. By fully focussing on improvement, Toyota dares to innovate and to think outside the box. A great example of this is the development of the Toyota Prius.

Toyota is one of the most successful car manufacturers of our time. In the US, the company is third on the list of bestselling car manufacturers. Toyota is a wonderful example of how diligence in business can take shape, how the customer can be put first and how a company can accept its responsibilities. Toyota's success story can teach us a lot about the growth of organisations and people and effective management. Thanks to the Kaizen principle, Toyota wins over General Motors. This is mainly thanks to the respect that the company has for its employees and customers. In the West we don't give respect much importance. Respect is not something you can learn, it is a feeling that you have to develop, or unwrap.

"Mr Gandhi, what do you think of Western civilisation?" a journalist once asked. Gandhi looked up, thought about it for a minute, thought about it a bit more, and then thought about it even longer. Then suddenly he said: "Ah, yes! That's a great idea!"

Toyota, constantly and step by step, introduces changes to the efficiency, quality and effectiveness of its products. These are small changes that are easy to implement. The risks are small. The overall effect of all these small changes is bigger than one big change. This touches on the Japanese way of renewal. We are in the habit of seeing old components as rubbish and we quickly and easily throw them away so that something totally new can be made. In Japan, renewing things means looking at how something that is new can be used to improve what is already there. Toyota's continuous quality improvement goes hand in hand with low production costs and high customer satisfaction.

The Japanese company's results don't lie. In the second quarter of 2010, Toyota made a profit of almost 1.7 billion Euros. It was the biggest net profit for two years. In the same period in the previous year there was a loss of 700 million Euros.

A good example of how they pay attention to their customers is Toyota's recall campaign. The car giant recalled more than ten million cars worldwide because of reputed problems with the gas and brake pedals. Toyota could have decided to cover up the problems and simply repair them during the first service at the garage but the company chose to be open about it. The recall measures were taken as a precaution.

Later it turned out that the problems with the cars in the United States weren't caused by technical defects but through mistakes made by the drivers. The fact that Toyota didn't use the outcome of this research to brag about how good they are, shows once again that Toyota has respect for its customers.

In the Netherlands, Toyota even brought in TNS NIPO, a renowned market research company, to get an insight into how satisfied their customers were about the way the company went about the recall campaign. The company purposely chose to do this at an early stage so that the reactions could be collected for Toyota drivers that had not yet been to the dealer. And what came out of the research on three thousand Toyota drivers? The Toyota dealer was given an average score of 8.6 for how they handled the recall campaign, 94.1% of the respondents indicated that Toyota had solved the problem well and 93.9% indicated that they still had every faith in Toyota. At the same time Toyota asked its customers for any other ways they could improve and some of these improvement suggestions have actually led to improvements. And despite the recall campaign, Toyota has still made a profit.

Cooperation determines the success of The Toyota Way, as Toyota's work method is called. Team spirit is extremely important in Japan and because of this the Japanese are very good at working together. They learned how to work well together by working the land to cultivate rice.

Only 35% of Japan is habitable and very few food crops can be cultivated. It all boils down to the fact that there is very little room. The staple food is rice; the Japanese also eat a lot of fish and vegetables but very little meat. As rice is so difficult to grow, the whole village had to help out.

The Japanese are used to a lot of social control. Their biggest fear is being excluded from the group. The fear of exclusion can have big consequences. Directors are known to commit suicide because of the shame brought on them when their company produces bad results.

Think as a team and show respect

The fact that we in the West could take Japan as an example does not mean to say that we should approach our business in exactly the same way. However, we can certainly be inspired by the approach of Japanese companies such as Toyota. It's all about picking out the good things and combining them with our Western approach. One of the good things is thinking as a team. In the West we are brought up to be individualistic. "Oh, I'll be long gone by then" is something you too often here. One of the most disturbing things in the Netherlands is the lack of respect for one another. It seems like many people think that they deserve more respect without having to be more respectful of others. This is also a typical example of egocentric behaviour.

Staff won't be inclined to leave a company where their voice is heard; even if they are offered a higher salary elsewhere.

尊重

You can practice respect. For example, in a company you can organise a so-called vertical meeting. Staff from throughout the company take part in the meeting, from the receptionist and the cleaners right through to the Director.

The hierarchy in this group is very different. It has nothing to do with the employee's job but rather the amount of time the person has worked for the company. A new staff member, even if he is in a leadership position and no matter how much knowledge he has, is lower in rank than an employee who has been working in a lower function for many years. The advantage of this kind of method is that you get rid of ego and arrogance. You enforce respect for people who have been working longer for the company.

Above all, as a company, you stimulate team spirit. Staff won't be inclined to leave such a company, where they are seen and heard, even if another company offers them a higher salary. In this way you add to the sustainability of a company.

Honda

Honda works following the shu ha ri principle. Shu stands for the form, working within a certain space. Because of the form there are boundaries. By working with the form and because there are boundaries you can evolve; that is ha. Once you have evolved you can let go of the form; that is ri. You are then the form.
Honda first develops the mould / the template. The development then takes place within that form. The mould is then released; the product is developed.

Mazda

In one of Mazda's television commercials, engineers are given the following assignment: make this car one hundred kilos lighter. You can't just simply remove part of the engine or the chassis. So what can you do? One of the engineers says: "Let's try to make each part just one gram lighter." That is looking at the whole picture. And, more importantly: it's creative. This kind of suggestion comes from the right side of the brain that you can only hear when you have a relaxed state of mind.
In another commercial it is clear to see that the door of a Mazda is very specifically designed because this is the first physical point of contact with a person. Isn't it wonderful to have the kind of mind that would realise this?

Western companies that have learned from Japan

Several companies in the West have tried to take on The Toyota Way. In 2006, as Chairman of the European Commission, José Manuel Barroso argued in favour of forming a connection with the East. That sounds easier than it actually is. We are not able to make the transition. In 1982 General Motors entered a joint venture with Toyota with the aim of taking on The Toyota Way. In principle this was a good idea, but it didn't work. The Toyota Way works or fails depending on the employees' development level. They aren't merely 'production machines', they all contribute towards a better car. This is always invested in. The staff at General Motors have never learned that, thus they don't know how to go about working in this new way.

This new work method involves many different things. At Toyota they see the improvement of work processes, services and products as something cyclical that is constantly in motion and within which the various parts all influence one another. In the West, improvement or innovation is often cut off from the whole and the discussion point is picked up in separate smaller project groups. By doing this, people within the company never really connect with one another.

Also, the work method has everything to do with respect. Respect is a feeling that you have to develop. It is not something you can learn, like holding your knife and fork. Having respect for your tea cup because you can drink tea from it is a deep feeling. Having respect for people, animals, nature and things will also make you feel at one with everything and everyone. The blood can only flow once there is a connection.

In Japan they also see making mistakes differently. In the West we dismiss staff for making a mistake. In Japan, what matters is that the work process is set up in such a way that the chance of a mistake being made is minimal. So, if a mistake is made, the work process will be improved and no one points a finger at the person who made the mistake.

In the West we think that we understand The Toyota Way but in actual fact, we really don't get it. Learning and knowing are not the same as understanding. If we Westerners want to learn how to understand, we first have to fully let go of the work methods we now know. Ishido sensei (a famous Master of sword fighting) says: "Before every lesson, let go of everything you've learned or think you have learned. Only then are you ready for a new – and for as far as this is possible: uninhibited – way of looking at things and only then can you learn something." Let's try to look – uninhibitedly – at a Japanese management method that is actively centred around people.

Bunsha – a practical approach

Bunsha is a well-known Japanese management method. It was devised some forty years ago and was developed by business experts, Kuniyasu Sakai and Hiroshi Sekiyama.[1] Whilst building up their business empire they discovered how, within their company, they could maximise profit, keep their staff productive and happy, and could make sure they had satisfied customers, with minimal input.

Bunsha is a principle based on maximum group sizing and literally means 'splitting up companies'. Also it focuses on stimulating intrinsic motivation, which is normal in the East.

A company shouldn't get so big that its main occupation is maintaining the status quo

The first thing that Bunsha stresses is that it makes no sense to let an organisation get bigger and bigger. A problem with many large (western) companies is that they grow too quickly. This isolates its leaders from the reality happening outside the Board Room. Because the company has grown too big, it loses its definition as a business. Just like a lumbering dinosaur it becomes less flexible and finds it difficult to adapt to changing situations. And situations have drastically changed in the last few years. In the Eighties, top managers saw themselves as the guy who sat at the head of the dinosaur that could still be steered a little bit. In the meantime top managers now find that the dinosaur can no longer be steered at all.

One of the basic principles of Bunsha is the need to achieve companywide innovation from time to time.

An employee can perform better if he is allowed to work independently and can coordinate his work how and when he wants, rather than being under someone's control. He gets more responsibility so his work becomes 'heavier', but the idea that he is at his own command and the pleasure that this brings, far outweighs this. Nothing is more stimulating than a person's desire for freedom. Bunsha uses this motivating power and channels it.

A company shouldn't get so big that its main occupation is maintaining the status quo. It should always focus on growth, but only on natural growth because the bigger a company is, the less its employees can contribute to its growth, resulting in a lack of motivation and involvement. Then intrinsic motivation comes into play. You can't solve this problem with seminars, courses, bonuses, extra holidays, etc. The downside to a company that is too big is that the employees have the feeling that they are no longer seen, and that is detrimental to one of the three basic incentives:

- ✓ Generic drive (80% of our behaviour can be put down to his)
- ✓ Wanting to feel good.
- ✓ Everyone wants to be seen and heard.

Through managed growth within a company, it will remain healthy so that employees will continue to want to make a contribution.

It is also less interesting for a manager to work for a company that is too big. What kind of manager wants to have to lead a thousand (or more) people that he doesn't even know, that makes products that he has no idea about how they work, and in factories that he has never seen? That is how they think in the East, but not in the West. Here, if you have a job managing lots of people, you are thought of as great. You are important ... But in actual fact, that is not the case. It is just what it appears to be from the outside.

So just how big can a company get? Anthropologist, Robin Dunbar, researched group processes and came to the conclusion that, for a group to be able to function well, it is important to recognise all of the interrelationships. The maximum number of relationships that a person can enter into is determined by the neocortex. This is the part of the brain responsible for our cognitive skills. Each type of animal can only maintain a limited number of relationships and the rule is: the bigger the neocortex, the bigger the number of relationships. Of all the different types of animal, the human being can take on the most number, that being one hundred and fifty. In former times disagreements would always arise where there was a group of more than one hundred and fifty people, which lead to an inevitable split off. Our brains haven't changed in the way they work over the centuries. For organisations, this means that when the number of employees exceeds one hundred and fifty, bureaucracy sets in. Complicated systems are needed to keep the organisation going. The bigger the group, the less efficiently it functions and the manager of such a group knows very little about what goes on on daily basis.

Employees work harder for colleagues that they know personally than for an 'unknown' from whom they receive an assignment. The bigger the organisation, the more e-mail is used as a form of communication. Normally, only 7% of communication is in the form of words, 38% is from the tone used when saying something and 55% is body language. When you talk to someone, you start up a connection. This isn't possible via e-mail. Direct communication saves a lot of trouble with interpretation and prevents having to put things right later on.

Instead of cutting costs, a company would be better off investing in something that the employee would get the most benefit from: a sense of achievement. Investing in human resources is enormously important. It sets the acquisition of knowledge and production in motion. The success of the organisation depends on its staff's performance and employees perform well when they feel good. Employees feel good when their talents are recognised and they have the freedom to make their own decisions. In short: staff performance goes hand in hand with 'empowerment': trust, respect and recognition.

A company should therefore only grow up to a maximum of one hundred and fifty employees. Further expansion is then possible, but only through natural growth. After all, the most natural way to grow is by dividing. There are more than enough examples of this in nature: animals, plants, the human body – they all grow through cell division. When a company becomes too large, it should be split up into smaller units. You end up with a conglomerate in which each company is fully independent and is even sometimes seen as competition by an affiliated company. But that is better than competing with a company outside the conglomerate.

The companies don't even have to share a group name in order to 'reassure' the customer; they are all stand-alone companies.

These smaller entities can take care of themselves much more easily. What they 'lack' in size and power, is more than compensated for by their mobility and adaptability, which gives them a bigger chance of survival. Growth is a natural process that we strive for, but only if it's controlled growth. You therefore achieve that by making parts independent once the company is healthy and moving forward, which will result in the new company starting up with a lot of energy and an enormous drive; the old company will then be revitalised by the reduction in staff numbers. An important consequence of splitting up a company is that new jobs and responsibilities are formed in both companies, which gives the employees new responsibilities and challenges. This increases intrinsic motivation yet again. Bunsha therefore creates the chance to advance growth and ensures that existing energy is still available for use and doesn't get lost.

A company's success is not always measured by its efficiency and the profit gained from it, albeit in the West it's all about shareholder value. The financial crisis has made it clear that this model doesn't work and it completely hollows out companies by denying the human side. A company can have more goals than just profitability, namely employment, education, a 'presence' in society, etc. People react more positively when they are made responsible for a set task. What is more important: targets set down by someone higher up or setting the goal yourself and achieving it? One of the disadvantages of outsourcing is that it limits the gathering and flow of information. Within each division of a company, if one person is responsible for the buying, another for the funding, and so on, their combined information network is much bigger than that of a centrally managed company, and that combined information network can be used by the whole division.

Another advantage of making part of a company independent is that it creates a challenging environment that brings out the best in people. Employees who are tired of their job and are just biding their time until retirement and only produce average work, get another lease of life. Responsibility and working together on something new within a competitive environment activates the spirit. An important issue when making part of a company independent is the support given by the parent company. This is needed until the split-off part of the company can stand on its own two feet. It is also essential that good leaders are appointed and that they are allowed to choose their own people. All of this is done to make sure that people come first within the company.

The importance of intrinsic motivation is one of the key issues of the Bunsha method. If an employee is independent and he can organise his own work instead of being under someone's command, he can perform better. Of course he gets more responsibilities and he will find that taking on the command himself is increasingly more enjoyable. There is no greater motivation for man than his desire for freedom. Bunsha makes use of this motivational power and channels it. Instead of lowering costs, you have to invest in what your employee will benefit from the most, and that is the feeling that he has achieved something. Trust, recognition and respect are the most important values for staff. The strength of this is that your employee can go home feeling proud after a hard day's work and having achieved what he wanted to achieve. And that is invaluable.

Therefore an atmosphere has to be created where an employee is not rewarded for the work that he does, but for pleasing his customers; because, what is also important, is that this has further economic benefits. Thanks to the customers, salaries can be paid so the least you can do is be good to your customer.

Ultimately, it is all about making sure that your employee is aware of the fact that what he does has a direct influence on the success of the organisation. The bigger the organisation gets, the more difficult this becomes.

A good leader knows the merits of each member of staff; he will give him as much responsibility as possible; and he creates a free atmosphere. People will enjoy their work through this; this isn't passive enjoyment (being entertained), but active pleasure, the pleasure from doing something. It doesn't matter how routine the work is, if a person feels fully involved in his work, there is always room for personal involvement. Should a company be the place where someone's spirit is broken, whilst the company flourishes? A company shouldn't be purely focussed on making a profit because it is also home to all of its staff. So it's not just about producing quality products and offering quality service but it is also about offering a good quality of life for its members of staff. After all, the employees are the driving force behind the company – and not the money.

Another advantage the Bunsha system has is that it offers employees room to grow, often quicker than would be possible within a conventional (western) company structure. Promoting your employees regularly is an important way of keeping the company young and dynamic. If you create a culture of mutual respect, everyone also feels safe enough to grow, and more importantly, to let growth happen. The manager is the centre point of these processes in Bunsha; each boss leads his people and encourages them.

The right process will deliver the right result.

We now come to an important point, that is the search for real knowhow. Most people have enough expertise or knowledge about their profession in an academic or scientific sense. What is really interesting is their knowledge of the process: how it should be done. This knowledge is usually only passed on from mouth to mouth. You could compare it to learning how to ride a bike. If you only know how to ride a bike in theory, you can't actually ride a bike yet. If you get on a bike without ever having ridden one before, you will fall off, for sure. Because of sequential thinking we are always a few steps ahead in our way of thinking. We aren't aware of the importance of preparation. The right process will deliver the right result. Success is in the preparation. This is where The Toyota Way comes in: the right procedure delivers the right results. In other words: focus on the process as it is right now and not on the result. In the West we do this the other way around, we only focus on the result. You can only build your knowledge of process, the knowhow, by actually doing it.

An employee who works using intrinsic motivation will perform more and better. It is all about motivating employees instead of merely (excessively) supervising them. Compassion for your employees is indeed a virtue, but excessive acceptance of their faults isn't. 'Fair but firm' is the motto. Only with this in place can there be freedom. Intrinsic motivation, as we've said before, can be used to support every employee in the company to give the feeling that he is creating something and that he is personally responsible for that creation. Then you will be a successful manager.

A good manager is someone who inspires others and tries to 'manage' them as little as possible. Strict supervision, control and bureaucracy suffocate the free spirit in a company. Instead of managing, you should lead: inspire your employees to perform better by letting them see how they contribute to the whole. You appeal (emotionally) to the most fundamental human need: to be needed, to be a part of a successful company. In the East everyone is focussed on finishing the job for a satisfied customer. This is the so-called organisational culture: the work is done thanks to a collective effort – the whole is more than the sum of the parts. Each employee excels himself through his performance.

Being taken on by the company is difficult, but being promoted from one level to another is much easier. This ensures that the employee also gets to know the company much better. On the other hand, in the West it is quite easy to be taken on by a company, but getting promoted to another job usually involves a long wait. The intrinsic motivation of employees ensures that their involvement and enthusiasm grows, that they take more initiative, and that the company becomes more innovative and processes are sped up. For this you need to have clear, continuous and involved communication between the top and the lower levels. You can make a clear distinction between management and leadership:

MANAGEMENT	LEADERSHIP
planning and budget	sets the course (vision)
strategic management of staff	inspires (for change)
ensures predictability	makes change happen

Table 1. The difference between management and leadership

As well as this, each manager has to delegate his authority as much as possible; this promotes motivation. After all, nine out of ten times, we control work by checking it afterwards. You can always question whether or not this has any added benefit. In the West, when a mistake is made, we always look to see who did it: in the East you learn to look at the system and to see how it can be improved. The eastern manager is chosen based on his development as a person, the western manager, based on his performance. You can question whether this is a real performance. Within the Bunsha system the manager knows his people (even the porter) at all levels and through this he is able to glean information at all levels within fifteen minutes. With this information he can make a sound decision that is good for the company and that reflects the real situation outside the Board Room.

What is the best way of communicating when there is going to be an important change in the organisation, according to Bunsha? By holding a ripple meeting (think of the ever increasing rings formed on water when you throw a pebble in a pond). It starts with the message being shared in a meeting with the Board of Directors. Then a meeting is held with the managers that report to the directors. The directors also attend this meeting. The same message is shared in this meeting as in the Board of Directors' meeting. Then it's the turn of the level that reports to the managers. They also hear the original message and the managers and directors also attend this meeting. The ripple meeting has a number of advantages:

The message is brought across more precisely, the more it is told.
The company gets an important insight into the reactions at the various levels.
Having heard the same message several times over, the Board of Directors is now beginning to understand the message really well.

Seen from an Eastern perspective, being a manager is clearly a dutiful task. There is no room for ego

What is crucial in the Bunsha process is the choice of leader for a company. He doesn't have a duty to the people above him, but to the people who work under him, the ones who (have to) trust him to make the right decisions and not to fail. This brings a strong sense of duty with it and sometimes he may have to turn a blind eye to his own leaders. A good manager doesn't surround himself with 'yes' men. A lovely illustration of a situation in which there is a sort of collective delusion within a group so that no-one dares to say anything is in Hans Christian Anderson's story, 'The Emperor's New Clothes.' In this story a vain Emperor walks around naked because none of his servants dares to say that they can't see his clothes. Two scoundrels have convinced him that the material his clothes are made of is invisible to people who are inexcusably stupid. Which manager would rather walk around 'naked' rather than having employees that can tell him what they think?

The manager is the face of the organisation to the outside world and it is expected of him that he will be the one working hardest for his customers. He has responsibility for every business relationship. It is expected of him that he can be trusted completely, regardless of the situation. From an eastern perspective, this is clearly a dutiful task. There is no room for ego here.

Ikiru was an abbot in Korewa, a monastery in Edo. One day the Governor of Edo visited him for the first time. The porter gave Ikiru the Governor's visiting card, on which was written: 'Dacho, Governor of Edo.' "I don't want to see this man," Ikiru told the porter, "tell him to go away." The porter took the card back apologetically. "Oh, that is my fault," said Dacho and he crossed off the words 'Governor of Edo' from his card. "Ask the abbot if he will see me now." "Ah, it's Dacho!" said Ikiru. "I do want to see *him*."

As a manager you should be very aware that you are an example to your employees at all times. Hiding yourself away in your office does you no good whatsoever; by simply walking through the corridors, lunching with your colleagues and showing customers around, you will have real contact with your employees. They can look at their boss and see from his manner (consciously or unknowingly) just what kind of mood he is in. You have to make a conscious decision to look like, and feel like, someone who enjoys his job. As a manager, the way you walk through the building really does matter. In the magazine, *Geld & Dienstverlening, Zo kan het ook! (Money & Customer Service, It can also be done like this!)(Nijgh Periodieken, September 2010)* consultant, Dien de Boer gives a great example of this. According to De Boer your hips have a lot to do with determining how you appear to others. Only when your hips are spread open and are moving is there room for expression and one can get a deep feeling as to who you really are as a person. A top executive had hips like concrete, even though he was otherwise quite an open person. He always stood and walked around as stiff as a board. Everyone looked upon him as a real boss and he was the one that everyone expected would solve the problems. He was tired out by all of this. De Boer taught him another, looser way of walking. The top executive tried it out. On one of the floors in the fifteen storey building where he worked, he walked around in the old way, then on another floor he walked in the new way. When he walked in the old way he was still asked to solve problems. In the new way, the employees enthusiastically invited him into their rooms to show him what they were doing and he heard their solutions and suggestions. He became extremely popular, now enjoys what he is doing and is no longer tired out.

More about the West versus Japan

We Westerners are far too focussed on the acquisition of new customers, increasing turnover and performance. How to please your customer so that he keeps coming back, buys more and/or gives you good publicity, is often forgotten. We are in a constant top state of willingness to perform, the result being that we constantly ask too much of ourselves, we become less creative and we no longer get any pleasure out of our work.

Performance is really a logical consequence of relaxation and then action at just the right moment. It's easy to think that you understand something because it is in your head. But at that stage you don't know it yet. It is only once your body has absorbed it that you really know it. You are then relaxed enough to be creative. Take hunting, for example: a hunter doesn't stand all day with his gun pointed, ready to shoot. He waits patiently in his hunter's lodge until the animal comes along. He then gets his gun and shoots.

In Japan, people work well together. Amongst other things, this can be put down to the fact that there is less fear of individual failure in the East. Being part of a group plays a much larger role there. You can depend on the group for safety. In the West we have a 'me, me, me' attitude with relationships around 'me'. In the East (Japan) you are not a 'me', you become a 'me' through the relationships that you have. The Japanese anthropologist, Satomi Ishikawa confirms this idea. In her thesis, 'Seeking the Self: Individualism and Popular Culture in Japan' she describes how the Japanese see themselves. Through teaching aikido, Ishikawa tries to help with the mutual understanding between Japan and the Netherlands.

The ultimate goal is to provide your customer with perfect service and thereby always being ahead of the competition.

In Japan innovation is something totally different to what it is in the West. For us it leads to a better end product and not to better work processes and internal communication or to better customer satisfaction. The ultimate goal is to provide your customer with perfect service and thereby always being ahead of the competition. When developing a new product, your starting point is your customers' requirements – the right process will deliver the right results. In the last decade, Japan has structurally spent more money on research and innovation than western companies. Using The Patent Power Scorecard from the American magazine, IEEE Spectrum, it appears that Japanese companies are making more progress with their patent portfolios than American or European companies. The magazine judged the research & development of 320 international companies using the patents that a company had in its portfolio. The list gives a view of the quantity, but more especially of the quality of the patents. Patents score high when they lead to new products and when they are often cited in other patent requests.

Compared to the 2007 list, the number of Japanese companies in the Top 320 has increased from 45 (14%) to 65 (20%). In the list of the Top 10 electronics companies there are seven Japanese companies. There are also seven Japanese companies in the Top Ten car companies. Two companies in the Top 3 of semi-conductor producers are Japanese. The number of European companies in the list is just the same as in 2007. It is expected that the American companies' shortcomings in the area of research and development will only worsen, given that they are cutting back on research and innovation costs.

Management and leadership are two notions that are often misunderstood. Whereas management is mainly involved with the managing of processes and employees, leadership is all about the freeing up of these things. Someone can develop into a true leader by clearly spreading the company's vision and by having an eye for an enterprise's real capital (its workers). There are a number of pitfalls for the modern day manager, including this one: by being too busy with managing and guiding and by not doing enough actual leading, it will have a negative effect on the work attitude and motivation of your staff.

In the West we have a fundamentally different view of people and work than in the East, as shown in Table 2.

East	West
Holistic	Partial
Inside world	Outside world
Harmony and integration	Gain and score
Leadership based on spiritual influence	Leadership based on results
Management through realisation	Management through organising a group and motivating people

Table 2. Eastern versus western view of work and people

These simple differences have made sure that western companies have mainly worked using these same principles for many years. In order to be able to bring in real change we would have to let go of these pre-conditioned ways of working and thinking and we would have to look outside our familiar, trusted box. The successful elements of western knowledge (product and market expertise) can then be combined with eastern wisdom. Everyone wants to be seen and have a share in the company. Pieter de Man, one of KLM's top managers realised that.

In a speech he named every employee by name. It was a long session, but no-one had a problem with that.

Leadership is keeping on top of your subject; a foreman who works alongside you is no good to you. It's all about 'digested knowledge', self made knowledge: someone who can provide the link between an individual and his intrinsic motivation. That leads to the utilization of human resources. Luckily the West increasingly has an eye for the 'soft side' of leadership. Referring to the rescue of mine workers in Chile, Professor Jan de Vuijst from the TiasNimbas Business School wrote a column about the added value of the power of encouragement.[2] Before they were rescued, the mineworkers were trapped in a mine for months. They survived thanks to two types of leader. Firstly, the formal leader, the foreman who was responsible for the group. He was also the last person to leave the mine. But it appears that there was also a miner who had natural leadership talent. He knew how to encourage the members of the group when they were threatening to give up. He then led them in prayer; he also set up a buddy system.

Another example of encouragement that De Vuijst quotes is about a troop of American soldiers in Vietnam. The soldiers were lost in the jungle, which changed around the formal roles. One soldier who could navigate by using the position of the stars, led the way whilst in the jungle. The commandant listened instead of giving orders. There was also an 'encourager' in this group. He made sure that the troop persevered when they were nearing exhaustion.

A totally different example is that of a handicapped man who, thanks to the encouragement of his daughter, was able to climb a mountain. The mountaineer had made several attempts at reaching the top of a mountain in the Seattle area. Despite the man's enormous willpower, he'd never managed it. Then, when his daughter went with him, he could do it. She safely steered him through a difficult glacier-like climb by constantly assuring him that he could do it and that he was the best father in the world. According to De Vuijst, that is the key to encouragement: the other person has himself to deliver the performance, but he has to know that he's not alone. He suggests that someone with a natural talent for encouragement is a very valuable team member. "A leader who has that talent, holds a powerful instrument: a vital element of charismatic leadership."

There are, of course, companies in the West that do combine East and West, even though there aren't so many of them, unfortunately. Here are two random examples.

Parmalat

The Italian dairy company, Parmalat, for example, was involved in an extensive fraud case that cost the company fourteen billion Euros. The new CEO, Enrico Bondi, had the job of putting the company back in order. He took a totally different approach to internal communication. He made it a requirement that employees made personal, direct contact with one another again; they had to have lunch together and the internal mail system was scrapped. Through this people got to know one another again. He also made it obligatory that everyone spoke to one another in a formal way. This approach was to bring back mutual respect. This policy has borne fruit: the company is now profitable again.

Virgin Atlantic Airlines

Businessman, Richard Branson, can also combine the best of both worlds. Branson wanted to fly from Great Britain to New York on business.

At the time there was only one cheap airline that flew that route. It was before we had internet so he had to call to book a flight. He called eight or nine times but two days later he still hadn't managed to get someone on the line to book the ticket. So Branson called his finance man with the announcement: "We're going to start a regular flight service to New York."

The finance guy promised to do some direct research and based on that he would make a report assessing all the opportunities and threats. But Branson would hear nothing of it. The conversation went something like this: "Believe me, I know that this is going to work because I've tried to call the only company that does the UK to New York route cheaply, but never got anyone on the line. This can mean one of two things: They are either very busy so there will be a market for us, or they are so badly organised that there is a market for us."[3] And this is how Richard Branson became the founder of Virgin Atlantic Airlines.

The leaders are the central point in these two examples. They've known how to combine the East and the West by heart and they are the example for their company showing how you can introduce true innovation and permanent improvements for customers and employees and how you can face obstacles. Also, a company's success blossoms or fails depending on the personal growth of its leaders, managers and employees. More insight into the Japanese way of thinking can contribute to this personal growth. So let's now look further into the source of Japanese knowledge.

有栖

Japanese knowledge – the Japanese sword, the source

To understand Japanese success it is important that we look at the source of their knowledge, the Japanese art of swordsmanship used by the Samurai.

Samurai

Samurai were aristocratic warriors, a kind of knight. They were attached to a Daimyo, a nobleman who in turn was attached to the Emperor and the Shogun. Only the Samurai were allowed to carry weapons.
The Samurai were more than just soldiers. They were fully engrossed in Zen, kept themselves busy with calligraphy and literature, and felt a true bond with their code of honour, the Bushido ('do' is 'way', 'bushi' means 'warrior'). Included in this code were: absolute dedication to the Daimyo, courage in all situations, and being prepared to die.

If there had to be a fight with the enemy, then each samurai sought out an appropriate contender by naming his family line, his teachers in the art of fighting and his achievements. His contender always had to be a challenge for him.

The Way of the Sword - Iaido

At the end of the Heian period (about 800 years ago), when the Samurai were in power – which they held for 700 years – they devoted themselves to personal development through practicing Zen. (Even today some large companies are run by Samurai families.) The result was that the art of fighting wasn't only a fighting technique, but it had a highly artistic, sensitive and spiritual content. The Samurai trained themselves in order to increase their ki (inner energy) with the help of meditation and breathing techniques.

The Yagyu family, who were privileged to have the Shogun (who held the highest rank in the Samurai command) to teach them in the art of fighting, made a distinction within the human spirit between an 'original spirit' (illuminated spirit) and a 'misled spirit' (one that is easily agitated by egocentricity and emotion). The Way of the Sword's basic aim was the development of an adult personality that wasn't influenced by a 'misled spirit' but which was formed through discipline and through expanding one's ki. This is the basis of Japanese leadership.

True practitioners of iaido strive towards enlightenment, harmony, serenity, purity of spirit and truth.

One difference from modern western combat sports is that, in the West, the accent lies on developing the body's physical agility and the muscles' capacity. The Japanese Way of the Sword is developed to strengthen the synthesis between awareness and unawareness by learning how to control one's tacit emotions.[4]

Iaido interprets the principles and concepts of Zen. Iaido is Zen in action. The words 'muga mushin' are an example of this. Loosely translated muga mushin means 'no self, no mind'. True practitioners of iaido strive towards enlightenment, harmony, serenity, purity of spirit and truth.
Their aim is to reach a spiritual level of calm where adversity no longer exists, before they die. This phase is called fudoshin.

In fudoshin, for one moment, body and mind become one and the person who achieves this is the strongest and cannot be mastered. He has to make use of this moment. If he doesn't, it becomes a moment of weakness, which gives his contender the chance to break his defence and to master the situation. Ultimately, the practitioner of iaido wants to achieve heijoshin.

This is peace of mind, a constantly stable state of being. To achieve this you need an awful lot of practice – a whole lifetime of practice. The iaido fighter trains his body, spirit, intellect, emotions and character his whole life long. He who achieves heijoshin before he dies, is a very happy person.

In the West, we think that we no longer have any career prospects once we turn 35, or that once we turn 65 we should take to our rocking chair, pipe and slippers – we think it's all over. In Japan you are considered to be middle-aged when you reach 60, and you peak somewhere between 70 and 80. That is only natural. If you have gained insight into what life is all about at that age, you are just in time. Even if you gain that insight just ten minutes before you die, you are just in time. Until that time ... just keep on training. 'Samurai' means 'those who serve'. In the Japanese art of swordsmanship it is all about the road that the fighters travel. This is also called shu ha ri. The Samurai learn how to work, live and understand using shu ha ri. It is a process of learning an art or a skill and making it your own. Shu ha ri is all about growth and the road to growth is seldom straight; it's usually winding. Each bend in the road stands for a positive or negative experience that the fighter has to learn about. Failure is just one step closer to success. Shu stands for the form, practicing within a limited space. This also means that the form is the beginning. You can't develop without boundaries. After shu comes the ha, the development. Thanks to the form, you can grow. In the end comes the letting go, the ri. You have become the form in your own, natural way.

The practitioner of the Japanese art of swordsmanship practices his adaptability skills so that he can react and move quickly and efficiently. Iaido is also called 'the true Way of the Sword'. The sword was used in the time of the Samurai to fight against a physical enemy. Nowadays you could compare the true Way of the Sword with our fight against the enemy within ourselves.

The essence of iaido is to win without baring your sword. If you can achieve that, it is a form of ultimate strength, courage and power. The iaido fighter distances himself from ego or showiness. He learns how to move simply and without effort.

To get from one side of the lake to the other, there is a little boat that brings the travellers back and forth. Two samurai sit in the boat. One of them is very loud and showy. The other sits quietly in a corner. After a while the bombastic samurai notices that the other samurai, sitting in the corner, has got a beautiful sword; he is secretly jealous of it. He says: "What good is such a beautiful sword to you if you are such a drip. And why have you got such a beautiful sword anyway ... which school are you from?" The humble samurai answers: "I come from the school of Win Without Fighting." "Never heard of it," says the bullfrog. "That can't be up to much. Come on, be a real man, I challenge you." It would take a while before they reached the other side of the lake and the samurai from the school of Win Without Fighting thought that the situation in that small boat could get out of hand. He said: "OK, I'll show you what I have learned. Halfway across the lake there is a small island. Let's hold our duel there." The bombastic samurai couldn't wait and the moment the little boat arrived on the island he jumped ashore and shouted. "Now I'll show you that you're a good-for-nothing and not worthy of such a beautiful sword." The samurai from the school of Win Without Fighting quickly picked up an oar and pushed the little boat back into the water.

Seppuku

In the West seppuku is better known as hara-kiri, ritual suicide. A samurai could choose for this if he wanted to avoid imprisonment or loss of honour. Seppuku could also be given as a punishment, but it was the most honourable form.

If the situation allowed it, a samurai committed seppuku just as he had fought: with full concentration. He prepared himself spiritually for it, then he sat down in the seiza position, bared his upper body, took a dagger and – preferably without showing any sign of pain on his face – he would slice his belly open in one fell swoop. Another samurai would stand by, ready to cut his head off at the moment when the pain was too much – and that moment was very hard to judge as he wanted to save him from pain, but at the same time he wanted to allow him to have his last moments of being.

In the past, ritual suicide could even higher the status of the next generations of a family. That is difficult for we Westerners to understand, but it isn't for the Japanese. They see death differently than we do. They don't see it as an end, as we do; they see it as a changeover into the following life.

Iaido focuses on the healthy development of the spirit (or mind), body and soul. The most important thing that the sword does, is to work in harmony with the body as we move from one movement to another whilst using the strength of our inner energy (ki).

The first 'I' in Iaido stands for the existence of the body and the spirit. The 'ai' stands for the ability to react and move quickly and efficiently.

A beautiful iaido phrase is 'muga mushin',
which loosely translated means
'no self, no mind'.

Nowadays, the true Way of the Sword is the fight against the enemy within oneself, such as ego, fear, anger and bitterness. By studying and practicing iaido, we expand our inner strength, which strengthens our character and makes us value our proud spirit (kigurai) more.

This is supported by the values that are bestowed on the folds of the hakema. This item of clothing has five folds on the front that stand for honour, humility, loyalty, justice and respect, and one fold on the back. We strive to attain all of the five values on the front so that we become the one on the back. They are all important values that ensure that we lead an honourable life. What we have to try to do is to protect those values as we learn to move the sword with a gracious simplicity, seriously and effortlessly – there is no room for flamboyant gestures or ego.

Iaido gives you the chance to not only become physically healthier, but also spiritually and mentally. Physically, we make sure we have strong legs, a powerful torso and posture and supple movements. The emphasis lies in the control, discipline, concentration and precision, skills that are developed by lots of practice.

Iaido is seen as one of the most spiritual martial arts, comprising the basic principles and concepts of Zen. The idea is to set aside any ego, swollen pride and thoughts of conquering one's opponent. The intention is to win without having to bare one's sword – that is the ultimate strength, courage and power.

True iaido practitioners are looking for enlightenment, harmony, serenity, clarity of spirit and truth. Just like the traditional Samurai, who were masters in their art of fighting, they are very courteous people who also keep themselves busy with painting, poetry, literature and philosophy.

Although the physical movements of iaido are complicated, the intention is to find simplicity to calm the spirit in difficult situations (fudoshin) – an extraordinary skill that iaido practitioners strive to learn. When the body sees a sword approaching, body and thought come together at the wink of an eye. There is no time for delay – a gap (the technical term is 'suki') – because that is seen as a weak point as it gives your opponent the chance to break through your defence and to take advantage of the situation.

The iaido practitioner's true path is to achieve heijoshin, 'presence of mind', a constant, balanced spirit. 'Hei'means 'flat, calm and stable'. 'Jo' means 'always, constant', and 'shin' means 'heart'- especially the mind, spirit and emotions – the true character. The basic principles of heijoshin are about the development of the spirit – the combination of intellect, emotions and character. Our inner spirit blossoms, just like a flower, thanks to exercise, patience and truth, when we take serious care of the people around us, at home, at work and in the dojo. This is true strength and beauty. Just like a flower that opens up slowly, before it is fully open; we have a whole life to develop our Iaido whilst striving for perfection – the ever moving target![5]

The sword

The sword is the Self, cutting through matter and time and penetrating into true insight.[6]

Making a sword

The cutting edge

Below the exquisiteness,
under the surface,
beneath the polish

deep within
the cutting edge
appendage

of this
cast iron blade,
dwell,
spirits of masters,
memoirs of seven centuries
and strict codes

In fine balance
it is almost weightless

having warded off
mud brown slides of
treacherousness
with one merciless gesture
thus justified

Breathing traditions of a not quite lost world
– GRETA CUNE

Cune wrote this poem after she'd held a sword from 1350 made by the smith, Morehisa.

According to legend the Samurai sword is the only sword that has a soul.. The Samurai swordsman handles it, not with force, but with speed and finesse. The sword is shock absorbent, flexible and razor-sharp. The unusual thing about a Samurai sword is that it is strong enough to cut through a person yet it is still a precision weapon. The manufacture of the Samurai sword is an art.

There are still as many schools for swordsmiths in Japan as there were centuries ago. The apprentices learn how to forge, shape and polish the sword, an art that is passed on from master to apprentice.

Thus, each swordsmith begins as an apprentice. Once the apprentice has mastered the basic principles, after years of practice and hard work, he can become a smith. Being a swordsmith is a spiritual way of life. The smithy is a spiritual place with an altar. The smith prays here every morning.

Forging the sword

The way the sword is made is surrounded by mystery. The swordsmith always dresses in white, just like the Shinto priests. The process of forging the sword takes place at a Shinto altar, using technical as well as religious rituals to complete the sword.

The kanji (Japanese symbol) for 'sword' has two components. One for the sword and one for the word 'combination'. A combination of what? We'll never know the answer to that question ...[7]

Testing the sword

To test the sword made by the Master Swordsmith, Muramasa, the owner of the sword held it in a stream, with the sword's blade facing into the flow of the stream.

A leaf floated by, brushed against the edge of the sword and purely through the strength of the stream, it was cut clean in two.

This test was seen as the ultimate proof of the quality of the sword until someone came up with the idea of trying it with a sword made by Muramasa's master, Masamune. The sword was put in the stream and a leaf floated onto the blade. At that moment, somehow miraculously, the leaf changed its course. It floated round the sword's deadly blade and continued on its way, completely unharmed. It was as if Masamune's sword held extraordinary powers and was much more than just a destructive weapon.[8]

Forging a Samurai sword is colossally hard work. You will not find a manual on how to assemble a sword on paper. The sword is made through following your feelings and based on experience, without using modern tools. The smith works by following his feelings, he listens to the fire. In the first phase, the steel from which the sword will be made is forged in the oven. The oven goes right down into the ground, so that no damp can get into the steel; that would ruin the quality of the sword. Once ten men have worked on the raw material non-stop for three whole days and three whole nights, it is then ready for the second phase and the oven is broken down in order to be able to get the raw material out.

The second phase in forging the sword is the shaping of the sword itself. The smith works the steel until all of the waste material is out of it. He hammers and folds the steel until he perfects the sword shape.

Then the sword goes to the polisher who makes it razor sharp. For this he uses special polishing stones; some are no bigger than a grain of sand. It is accurate work that can be extremely perilous.

The finished sword is soft and flexible so that it won't break. At the same time, the sword is hard and sharp so that it can cut things easily.

The sword is the indicating stick that shows precisely what your body is doing, up to the very last millimetre. It teaches you how to move your body in a natural way. Empty your head and then it will just happen. The sword exposes your inner conflicts.

The dojo

The dojo is the training hall and the battleground. Originally, the dojo was a Shinto sanctuary with an altar, the kamiza. In this way, training and fighting are given a spiritual character. The word 'dojo' can be translated in many ways. I think the best translation is 'place of awakening'.

In the training hall – the dojo – there are rules that everyone has to abide by. The rules in the dojo set boundaries. One of the rules in the dojo is about respect.

When you enter the dojo, you bow towards the kamiza, the spiritual centre of the dojo, and by doing this you are also bowing to everyone who has been on the Way of the Sword before you. Thanks to their efforts, the knowledge is still around and can be passed on. The art of fighting is a living art. If it were no longer practiced, it would be lost. Knowing how to bow well is an art. It has to come from the hara (see Dürckheim's *Hara, the Vital Centre of Man).* In the West you see that everyone bows with their head. This isn't surprising when you know that we do things mainly with our head – that is where you will usually find us. Some people find it very difficult to bow. Their ego gets stuck between their chin and their belly. They can't bow. That's not so handy.

In the art of swordsmanship in Japan, bamboo is the symbol of life. The sections (or internodal regions) of the bamboo stand for the different phases of life. The fact that it grows up straight into the air is a symbol for our body posture, standing straight. Only then is everything linked to one another and the energy can flow.

In every life there are a couple of heavy storms, in business as well as private life. If you are not able to bow as bamboo does, there is a chance that you will break. And then you won't be able to get back up again. Try again in your next life! Bamboo really is strong and flexible so that when the storm calms down it can get back up again.

At the start of the lesson, the pupils bow to their teacher (sensei). By doing this, they are bowing to the past. The teacher bows to his pupils at the same time. He is bowing to the future. And the passing on of knowledge happens in the here and now.

There are a lot of behavioural rules in the dojo. In the first instance, to provide for a safe and respectful way of treating one another during the training. After all, you are being trained in potentially lethal techniques. In the second instance, to facilitate the passing on of knowledge.

This isn't only done through words, but especially through resonance and connection. Also training a lot in a dojo contributes to your being able to get a quicker grasp on real knowledge (Rupert Sheldrake's 'morphogenetic fields').

Rei

When you start on the Way of the Sword, you can question whether your journey conforms with what you have already learned in the area of religion. You can even question if there are really any religious elements to the Way of the Sword. What the beginner doesn't yet know is that there is a difference between religion and spirituality. The Way of the Sword is not linked to any religion. The Way of the Sword gives you a better in-road to any religion. The only condition is that you have to focus on spirituality and part of this focus comes out in rei (etiquette).

In the Middle Ages there were a lot of things written, describing rei. Rei was needed to be able to cope with the frictions that arose when samurai met one another off the battlefield: for example, there are descriptions of how you should enter a room, but also how you should hand over your sword in the presence of others, how to sit and how to stand up. Everything is focussed on avoiding conflict or a threatening, aggressive stance. Of course rei also offered protection. Thanks to this etiquette you can move and interact with others without being in danger of exposing yourself.

The classic martial arts have incorporated a great deal of this etiquette. All samurai knew and practiced this etiquette. You can even see where someone comes from and which style he practices through this etiquette.

In Japan rei has become a part of the collective sub consciousness. Rei is a vital part of Japanese culture. The basic notion is that if everything is clean and proper on the outside, it should also be so on the inside. If it's a beautiful shadow, the pattern that created the shadow must also be beautiful. In Japan, where a stoic posture when facing the outside world is considered very important, rei, if you've got it in you, is a good way of exercising self control and a way of protecting your spirit.

Rei is a question of presence. Rei gives you privacy. Rei is covering up your emotions. Someone can be furious deep down, but from the outside there is no sign of it so you can totally confuse the enemy.

Rei is of enormous importance for every serious student in the Way of the Sword. In the dojo, rei determines how you move, how weapons are handed over, etc. when you are training with real weapons, in order to avoid accidents.

Rei puts a framework around the soul to support and protect. In the Japanese character, rei is shown as a man who kneels before the altar. Rei teaches you how you should sit in front of the altar. It is left to the person sitting at the altar to decide what he'll do there, practice his religion or spirituality.[9]

Martial arts without etiquette is nothing more than bravado, the opposite is barbarity.[10]

Training doesn't only take place within the walls of the dojo. Training is done everywhere.

Japan developed as a country and as a culture in a way which is decidedly unfamiliar to the ways of the West. And so your journey is much more difficult than it would have been if you had just decided to study a Western art with the same intensity and exertion. To be absolutely precise, it is a big task or journey that you have to keep travelling and researching. It is no easy path that you are following. But you can take it because if you do you will see many views, learn about many concepts, discover many truths, whereas those who are not inclined to follow such a path, will never know these things.[11]

The dojo offers no escape from everyday life but it is more of a place where we face the pent up problems in our daily life and learn how to deal with them.

The term 'iai' is taken from the phrase 'Tsune ni itte, kyu ni awasu.' The meaning of this is, whatever we may be doing or wherever we may be, we must always be prepared for any eventuality.

Through the sword we seek to improve our spirit and become better people, to promote peace and good feeling beyond the walls of the dojo and into our daily lives. There are so many styles of iai, many ways to cut, to move and as one learns, one improves technically. However, we train not only to learn techniques, but also to cultivate the heart and spirit, and in this respect all 'styles' lead to the same goal.

One must bear in mind the higher goals to achieve and take each step and overcome each obstacle, but at the same time, though the path may be a difficult one to follow, one must relish and enjoy the challenges.

– Haruna Matsua Nanadan Kyoshi, december 1994[12]

In the West we are used to asking questions; preferably before we even start on something. Iaido works the other way around. Pupils ask nothing, they just do it. Only when they have trained a lot may they ask the iaido master questions. That is because you can only ask good questions when you know what you are doing. Pupils learn that you have to train a lot before you can start to gradually understand something and that knowledge is no good if you don't have it in you.

The iaido master's answer is not always what the pupil expects. Sometimes he just says: "Train even harder." The strength in training is in the repetition. And repetition requires patience. Patience is something that we Westerners often lack. We always want to move on; move on to the next part, a new chapter or another project. This results in our always bobbing about on the surface. Impatience is the consequence of misunderstanding.

Being patient

Haiku on a Japanese nightingale

If the hototogisu (Japanese nightingale)
doesn't sing
then ...

The first man to have a large part of Japan under his governance was Oda Nobunaga. He was a tyrant with an ego, who killed anyone who got in his way. Once he'd reached the very top, it didn't take long before one of his own men got him out of the way. If he had been able to complete the haiku, it would have gone like this:

If the hototogisu
doesn't sing
then ... kill it.

Nobunaga's successor was Toyotomi Hideyoshi, a clever peasant who only got on well at the expense of others, through elbowing them out of the way. He was really unhappy at Court in his role as regent as he was never fully accepted by the aristocracy and intelligentsia. If he had been able to complete the haiku, it would have gone like this:

If the hototogisu
doesn't sing
then ... try to make it sing.

Toyotomi Hideyoshi also quickly disappeared from the scene. Ieyasu Togukawa then came to power. He had suffered losses and had some success. He had learned a lot and he had a good overview of things. Togukawa set up a dynasty that would remain in power for 268 years. If he had been able to complete the haiku, it would have gone like this:

If the hototogisu
doesn't sing
then ... wait.

Togukawa practiced being patient by travelling to a meeting on a turtle's back ...'[13]

Training

It is important to practice marubashi (to smooth off the sharp edges of your spirit), not only for the technique of how you should hold your sword, but also to make your spirit marubashi.

A person has a lot of sharp edges. By practicing iaido we try to make the sharp edges of our way of thinking rounder. Once we have worn away our way of thinking into a circle ('wa' or harmony), only then can we become a real samurai.

Always try to be better today than you were yesterday.

– Matsuoka and Kinomoto sensei, august 2005

You can't just become an iaido fighter, just like that. You need intense training for it. One of the most difficult parts of that training is that you no longer have to think, you just have to do it.

Posture and movement

Stretch your neck, drop your shoulders and tighten your buttocks, but keep the tension out of your legs so that the body can find it's natural balance.

Your legs will automatically and naturally fall into place from your hips being in the right position.

Having your eyes fixed resolutely on the horizon is essential for the stability of your body.

When moving, your arms should always follow your legs; the legs never follow the arms.

The distance between your feet is more or less the same as the grip on your sword.

If you are using your sword only in your right hand, then your left hand makes sure that your body is in the correct position. Handle the sword's sheath in the same way as you would handle the sword.

Stay calm. Find the moment of action in tranquillity and tranquillity in the moment of action. Always act as if you are dealing with an enemy who is stronger than you are. Don't walk too quickly; that is a sign of excitement. Don't walk too slowly; that is a sign of weakness. Walk with a calm step that shows no excitement or fear.[14]

The four most important aspects of training

Relaxed and tensed
Know when you have to tense up and when you can relax. It sounds so easy, but it isn't. It is a process of awareness that needs maintaining. The basic factor in becoming aware is listening to your body.

Look after your body
You have to look after your body by exercising but also by relaxing. The iaido practitioner needs a healthy body. The training sessions give him strong legs, a strong torso and posture. He trains to gain flexible movements by using control, discipline, concentration, precision and repetition of the exercise. The sword is an extension of the body and mind; both work together in harmony. The movements of the sword flow into one another using inner energy, ki.

Here also, we see how important the body – the receiver of messages – and the right state of mind (alpha waves) are.
Above all, the body doesn't lie and gives off useful signals – for the practiced eye of the iaidoka.

Balance

Another important part of the iaido training is balance. The iaido fighter is master of all situations if he is in balance. He strives to bring his body and mind in balance. Iaido is therefore about awareness, concentration and a peaceful mind. It is therefore not seen as a sport but as a unique and ancient traditional art to develop the body, mind and soul. Integrity is also part of the iaido training.

You cannot control a situation,
but you can learn to master it.

Kata

'Kata' means 'form'. Form is the beginning. Form creates boundaries. Without boundaries you cannot develop and you will keep drifting endlessly. Once you have developed fully, then you can let go of the form. In practice (iaido) this means that you have united your body and mind so that you are 'natural'.

Technique

Iaido has 84 kata that can be summarised in the following basic techniques:

Baring the sword, leading straight away into a cut (nikitsuke).

The immediately following blow, cut or stab (kiritsuke).

If the opponent is cut, the blood is cast off the blade of the sword (chiburi).

Placing the sword back into its sheath (noto).

It is interesting that with these four techniques you can take on any fighting situation! Just by being able to do one thing well (the four basic techniques), you are in a position to be able to understand everything. The secret is doing it 'naturally'. By understanding the nature of things, you can see the patterns and arrangements. You can try to push back the sea at high tide, but it won't turn back the tide ...

Learning well from one is the way to understanding all.

The swordsman

The iaido practitioner performs his movements with the sword fluently, flawlessly and resolutely. He reacts quickly to attacks by one or more opponents. They can come from the front, behind and the side. He receives the attacks from a sitting or standing position. He has to be fully concentrated and alert.

The aido practicioner always fights against an enemy, even if there isn't one there in a training session. He then imagines the enemy to prevent iaido becoming a mechanical act. You can only practice iaido when you give it your full attention. It's all about actually doing it, not the result.

Rhythm

An important lesson from the art of Japanese swordsmanship is about rhythm. Nature is clearly present in the rhythm and the timing of the Eastern martial arts practitioner. In contrast with the regular rhythm of the boxer or the speedball, the cadence of the movements of an Eastern martial arts practitioner is never even. The cadence is perpetually varied in its movements, pauses, moments of perfect silence and outbursts of action.

Hyoshi is written with two characters. 'Hyo' means 'hand' and 'clap'. 'Shi' is kanji for 'child'. Thus, a child that claps. Rhythmically rough, irregular and unpredictable.
The advantage for an experienced practitioner of Eastern martial arts is therefore that, through being 'natural', he is in the right state to be able to manipulate his timing. When he moves, it is as surprising as thunder. When he pauses, a frozen silence falls all around like the calm before the storm.
Only the truly spiritually developed opponent can withstand the desire to oppose this, thereby preventing himself from reacting and making himself vulnerable, which would mean losing.
In order to perfect your timing you use sei and do. Movement and rest. Learning correct timing is the first step on the way to understanding and feeling rhythm and life itself.[15]

Buddhism and Zen

In Japan they have kept the feeling that man is one with nature, unlike in the West.

Movements that propagate and help advance this awareness (being aware) are Shinto, Buddhism and Zen. Buddhism originates from around 500 BC in India and became known in Japan around the time when we started our calendar. (Japan also has Confucianism, as well as many others). Buddhism knows many different movements, even within Japan. The common denominator of these movements is introspection.
Zen is originally a Buddhist movement from China (chan). It also has many different movements. The common denominator of these is introspection by doing things attentively, in the here and now, as the only solid reality.

Letting go of preconceived ideas

The essence of Zen is letting go of all preconceived ideas, images, ideas, opinions and thoughts that you have collected throughout your life, which mean that you can no longer see clearly.

Perception: the story of the Master Archer

The Japanese Shogun was riding through Japan with his men and he suddenly came across a small village. Everywhere he looked, there was a target with an arrow going exactly through its middle. In the trees, on the roofs, on water barrels, on doors. He was instantly fascinated. A Master Archer must live here! He ordered one of his samurai to seek out this Master Archer and to bring him to him. No, thought the Shogun, seek him out and I'll go to him. Half an hour later the samurai returned with the news that he had found the person who had shot the arrows. Before the samurai could get his words out, the Shogun shouted: "Bring me to him!"
They rode through the village and came across a small house. The samurai knocked on the door and a young boy of around ten years old answered. The Shogun said: "Boy, go and fetch your father, the Master Archer!"
The samurai said: "Uh ... Shogun, this boy is the one who shot those arrows ..." The Shogun was deeply impressed.

He said: “Master, may I invite you to Court and would you please teach me? But before we go, would you tell me how you could possibly shoot all your arrows so precisely into the bulls eye of those targets?”

The boy looked somewhat embarrassed and stammered: “Well ... uh ... you see ... uh ... I shoot an arrow ... and then I draw a circle around it ...”

Zen teaches you to look clearly in the here and now and to expand your awareness (after all this is one of the conditions for change!). You need your body and your mind for this. So you have to sit properly, breath properly, and so on. Do that consciously; frequency comes after dedication. It is better to do something once a week consciously, than six times a week inattentively.

Zen sets itself aside from Buddhism: If you are a long way on with your development and you have a vision of Buddha, then you are given the advice: “Kill the Buddha.” After all, your image of Buddha is only an image.

Ki

‘Ki’ is the Japanese word for what we know as ‘chi’. Ki is life force. According to the Japanese, it enters you in your lower stomach, a few centimetres under your navel, in the hara. The influx of ki can be purposefully expanded with the help of meditation and exercising your body. In Japan, ki has been used for healing since around 500 AD. Ki is of course very important within the many martial arts that Japan has, for the body’s balance as well as for the energy used when grasping, lunging or striking.

There is a constant dialogue with ki. Everything is constantly developing, therefore so are ki, people and their relationship to one another.

What you learn from the Way of the Sword

Proactive behaviour
The sword teaches you to act, rather than react. Through this you can continue working under your own steam (strength) and you stay on top of the situation – you master it.

Everyone can do something. But not everyone can guarantee success.

Breathing
Your breathing always occurs in the here and now. Life is only available in the here and now. Through connecting yourself with your breathing, you come into the here and now.

Here and now
This is the only moment where life is.

Rest
The sword teaches you that all action starts from being rested and through this it can be natural and successful.

Feel comfortable when you have an uncomfortable feeling.

Speed from the subconscious
The sword teaches you that the body's wisdom is exponentially bigger than the brain's intelligence. The body knows what it has to do.

Letting go of hindrances
Trust nothing that isn't divine.

The sword teaches you that it's the intention that matters
Do your best and let the heavens decide.

Pure perception
The sword teaches you to peel off your layers of conditioning so that you can ultimately see things as they really are.

Four samurai stood on different sides of a mountain and described the mountain as they saw it. They each described the mountain in a different way. It was only when they had climbed the mountain and they were all standing on the top of it that they all saw the same thing: the moon.

Confidence
You have to have confidence in order to be able to do things. Without confidence you are passive. Realisation and grounding bring you into the here and now.

Doing less
If you are so far advanced that you have confidence and you do things, then start doing less!

Development
Iaido teaches you to be able to see. A lot of things are 'miegakure', which means 'deliberately hidden', 'out of normal sight'. Through training a lot, realisation and a deeper awareness come to light. Through this you learn how to see better, so that what at first appeared to be hidden, now becomes visible.

The concepts help you to find the right answer through your own efforts and in every situation in an ever changing world. They help you to function with more pleasure and less stress and strain, they lead you to inner peace and offer insight. You no longer have to make an effort to achieve success, you can just relax.

Ikiru sensei sat with his best friend, Watanabe sensei, talking about which one of his sons would succeed him as Grand Master in the art of swordsmanship. Together, they thought up a test to see who would be the most appropriate.

They sat waiting in the dojo and they had placed a vase on top of the door. It wasn't a regular sliding door, but a door that had to be pushed open from the outside.

First they called for Hiroshi, the youngest son. He came storming in, the vase fell straight onto his head but before the vase could hit the ground, Hiroshi had pulled out his sword and sliced the vase in two.

Once Watanabe sensei and Ikiru sensei had found another vase and had put it on top of the door, they called for the oldest son, Oda. He came in, spotted the vase just in time and caught it, thus preventing being harmed.

Lastly, they called for Ieyasu, the middle son. When he reached the door, he stood still for a moment. He opened the door a little, caught the vase in one hand, stepped over the threshold, closed the door behind him with his other hand, put the vase on the ground and greeted the two Masters.[16]

Overview of Iaido concepts for a healthy and successful life[17]

Enzan no metsuke
Looking at a distant mountain. This means that the eyes focus on one point in the distance, giving you a broad field of vision, your natural way of looking, 270 degrees. Don't just stare blindly, but see everything.

You need this in your work life to be able to develop a long term view, to have an overview so that you can see the difference between the symptoms of a problem and the problem itself, and so that you can ensure that everyone stays on track, as a leader.

Fudoshin
This is the 'immovable mind': when the mind is free to be able to see all things as they are and it is unhindered by preconception and doesn't get stuck to one particular thought.

To be able to provide leadership you have to have a clear view to be able to develop a vision that will benefit the company.

Fushin
The hindered mind. If you are led by fear or doubt, or you are distracted by logical and conceptual thinking, the mind isn't free to react to situations.

In the West everyone is stuck in a way of sequential thinking and doesn't live in the here and now, because of which it is difficult or impossible for us to react adequately.

Jo ha kyu
Describes action in detail. Soft, smooth and sharp. Preparation, development, conclusion/completion. All natural processes follow this path. 'The speed is at the end' is a part of jo ha kyu. The relevance is in the timing: a gradual speed-up with a feeling of increasing pressure up to a maximum, after which the movement stops.

By only thinking, we are often at the result stage already and we forget the preparation and the gradual speeding-up.

Kokoro
The state of fairness and integrity that makes sure there is trust and respect.

Essential for a leader.

Tai shi tai bun
Think with your body, listen with your body (and not with your brain and ears). Trusting your ears and brain to absorb information is shallow.
Thinking rationally about a technique is irrelevant. You have to feel swordsmanship and it has to be absorbed through your whole body, by learning, doing and being.

A real leader shows his leadership through what he does and not through what he says.

Kokorogamae
Mental state. Calm focus, metsuke (all-seeing), spirit, alert, concentration, timing and distance. This is the attitude of a swordsman and a true leader.

The influence on work life

It is clear that Japanese companies that are aware of the source of their knowledge, and know how to adapt this to fit their own enterprise, have a whole other view of doing business, focussed on the long term, on continuity and on collectivity. Japanese enterprises like Toyota or Honda start with bonding, natural growth and improvement of work processes – where everyone contributes their little bit. Through this the work makes more sense.

At Toyota, the Way of the Sword forms the basic platform for the enterprise. First the long term vision is decided upon. This vision doesn't have an end goal, it is a process with a beginning but no end. Then the right work processes are put in place, through which there is confidence that the right processes will lead to the right results. All employees (kaizen) then add their value to this process and the contribution of all the employees to this process is valued. With this as a basis, all core problems can then be solved or new challenges can be introduced. In the next chapter, we will examine how we in the West can use the Japanese source of knowledge, as outlined in this chapter, in our everyday practice.

道場

有栖

How do you achieve success? Japanese lessons in practice

Un-wrapping

To develop means to un-wrap – to take the wrapping off. How does that work?

If you look at your life as a film and you stop the film for a moment, then it will look like it is made up of lots of different frames. Each frame is about an event in your life. When you think about some of these events, it makes you feel tense – usually a negative tension. This tension is linked to this experience, to this frame.

Now your brain (the limbic part of your brain) is working in a way that, if something happens in your life that also reminds you in some way of something that happened in the past, the limbic part of your brain automatically brings up the 'old frame' and it's almost as if you are experiencing it – in terms of the tense feeling – all over again. This is a subconscious process but you can recognise it in that it does make you think: why do I always feel this way?

And so when you re-experience something subconsciously, you pile on yet more tension.

The aim of swordsmanship is to neutralise all of the frames so that you can be open, and open minded, in the here and now. Then you can make a good cut. This is only possible when there are no longer any inner conflicts in the way. That is why it is also said: "We cut through the air to be clear on the inside." (Iaido is practiced without an opponent, mainly for safety reasons. This makes it a lot more difficult because you have to imagine a realistic opponent and the fight has to be 'real'. You can only do this by going deep down into yourself.)

Iaido is also called 'Zen in action'. What is Zen, actually? Zen cannot be expressed in words. It is all about feeling, experiencing and reflecting. You just have to know it! To give you an idea, you could say that Zen lets you see things as they are ...

The process of development, Zen and iaido can be explained to some extent by using a model of the four layers of consciousness, used in western psychology. Again, it is only to give you an idea about it, as really it's more about actually experiencing it and feeling it with your body, not about thinking.

We can distinguish four layers of consciousness (in the East they use a model with nine layers).

Layer 1.
Personal consciousness. This is the layer holding all of the positive and negative experiences / frames that you have had today, from the moment you woke up.

Layer 2.
Personal sub consciousness. This is the layer holding all of the positive and negative experiences / frames that you have had from the moment you were born.

Layers 1 and 2 have an influence on one another. Experiences from the past will (subconsciously) steer your behaviour today, and the experiences you have today will have an influence on your sub consciousness and therefore on your future behaviour.

Layer 3.
Collective sub consciousness. This is the layer holding your archetypes, your notion of good and bad.

Layer 4.
Cosmic sub consciousness. This is the layer that puts you into the state of being conscious of the mystery of being, or put in an easier way: you are aware that there is more between heaven and earth (but you don't know exactly what).

Under these four layers there are the Source, the Self, God, Allah, Buddha, Vishnu, Energy, etc.

Iaido's work is to clear up all of the frames that disturb the picture and ultimately to take you down so deep into the layers that you can make contact with what is (in a matter of speaking) under the fourth layer.

When you have neutralised your frames, you have cleared up all of your adverse images from the past and the past has lost its power over you. So you are free to be. In the here and now. Tai shi tai bun: think with your body, hear with your body, instead of with your brain and your ears. Trusting your ears and your brain to absorb information is superficial. Thinking logically about a technique is irrelevant. You have to be able to feel the art of swordsmanship and it has to be absorbed into and through your whole body by learning through doing and being. The body has to do the work. The wisdom of the body is exponentially bigger than the intelligence of the brain.

The Heart Sutra says the following about the result of this process:

Oh, Sariputra, all things are marked with emptiness (meaning, connected to one another). They have neither a beginning nor an end, they are untainted and not untainted, they are not complete and not incomplete. Therefore, oh Sariputra, in this emptiness there is no form, no perception, no name, no conceptions, no knowledge. No eyes, no tongue, no mind. No form, no sound, no smell, no taste, no touch, no objects. There is no knowledge, no ignorance and also no elimination of it. There is no old-age nor death; there are no four truths, that is to say, there is no suffering and no path leading to the extinction of it. There is no knowledge of Nirvana, nor any chance of attaining it, but also of not attaining it. Therefore, oh Sariputra, as man can't attain Nirvana, he who has approached the complete enlightenment of the Bodhisattva, has uninhibited consciousness

When the inhibitions of consciousness are destroyed, man is relieved of all fear, change has lost its grip on us, while man may look forward to at last achieving Nirvana.

The two halves of our brain

How do we bring the East and the West together? By cherry picking. We have to gather the pearls of wisdom from the East and combine them with our working methods. The source of the knowledge lies concealed in the Way of the Sword. And the secret of the sword's strength lies concealed in the five thousand year history that is within yourself. Perfect harmony connects the sword and man. In the West we can learn from the East, especially from Japan. The various management styles, but also the way that people live their lives, can help us.

In the East people are more in balance. Japan is called the land of wa;

‘wa’ means ‘harmony’. In the West we are rarely in balance. We only believe in our reason and we have lost the bond with our perception, our intuition.

It is supposed that reason resides in the left side of the brain and intuition, creativity and emotion in the right.

Our brain has two halves with a bridge between them. Just for the image, you could say that there is a gateway on that bridge. That gateway has the biggest capacity when the vibrations that go through it are in the alpha area; this is also called flow. You are standing under the shower and something comes to you all of a sudden – pow! In the beta area (when it is busy in your head) the gate is firmly shut. The trick is to manage this area. Top sports people, musicians, Board members, they can do this. That is called peak performance. That means, if you are under a lot of pressure, you are still capable of keeping relaxed with the right side of your brain fully participating.

The challenge for the West is to more actively use the right side of our brain.

Imagine this: you want your employees to solve a problem. You split them into two groups. You send the first group off to brain storm and come up with solutions. Two days later they are dog tired. You tell the second group: “Tomorrow morning, come to work a bit later, say ten o’clock.” You give them a warm welcome when they arrive then casually, at some stage during the day you say: “Oh yes, please would you have a read through this story and then you can go home. Come and see me tomorrow at, let’s say, round about four. But apart from that, take the day off on paid leave." Then the next day you also casually enquire: "Oh yes, did you get chance to think of a solution to that problem?" The number of solutions for the second group will be significantly higher than that of the first. This is an example of how the right side of your brain works and that you can tune in to the alpha side of your brain.

It is a bit of a paradox: by slowing down you can achieve more, just like in the art of swordsmanship. This conflicts with our Calvinism. The biggest impediment is fear. If I slow down, I'm going to feel things, I'm going to live, and that scares a lot of people because they don't know how to cope with it. You have to learn how to feel. Iaido.

You, when relaxed, that is who you are. In the West we have strayed away from who we are. We learn to mainly use the left side of our brain. Thereby, according to psychologist, Ab Dijksterhuis, we only use a seventh of our capacity. However, Asian people, traditionally, make more active use of the right side of their brain. In the East, body and mind are not set apart from one another but the people there, for some five thousand years already, have been aware that body and soul are one and that they are linked to their surroundings. As we have said already, the wisdom of the body is exponentially bigger than the intelligence of the brain. We in the West are now finding this out scientifically. The challenge for the West is to make more active use of the right side of our brain. We seldom listen to this side of the brain. If we use both the left and the right sides of the brain, we will be more able to cope with the enormous amount of information that we are faced with every day. Research done by Dr. Tadanobu Tsunoda, an authority in the field of the functions of the brain, points to the fact that English is a language that uses the left side of the brain, and Japanese uses the right side.

The left side of our brain has provided we Westerners with an awful lot. It has brought us prosperity through our seemingly being more productive. It brought us medical science and a higher life expectancy. It is worthy of note that we measure the prosperity of a country using Gross National Product. Taken literally, GNP shows us a country's production and nothing more. But we have wrongly made a prosperity quotient of it. The Netherlands, for example, has one of the World's highest GNPs. But what does this say about prosperity? It is significant that in countries with high GNP, more people take anti-depressants, more people have cancer and there are more structural disasters, like collapsed bridges. The GNP of Western countries has been rising for years, whilst the residents of these countries admit to feeling increasingly unhappy.

We are so fixed on reason, with so much going on in our heads, thoughts shooting back and forth, that we may feel stressed or burnt out. We don't trust our own wisdom and our inner voice because we have been taught to think and make decisions rationally. But even we Westerners have at one time or another had the idea that our gut feeling tells us one thing and our mind tells us another. But we then denied our feeling and listened to reason ('that's a load of rubbish – it doesn't make sense'). Usually, it turns out that we should have listened to our gut feeling.

"Men are disturbed not by things, but by the view which they take of them," said Epictetus. This statement is of course all about perception and learning how to see things. And that is what Zen is for! That is why old people are so respected in Japan, because they have learned how to look at things; enzan no metsuke (looking at a distant mountain) is needed for an overview of everything (so that you can see the root problem and the long term vision).

Age

When practicing the art of swordsmanship, young people throw their energy around. Older people don't; you see things just naturally falling together when they do it. They do more with less energy. You'd also like to see that happening in the business world. In the West you are written off when you are thirty five. In Japan you peak at seventy. The added value of people with experience – as long as they still have an open mind – is, of course, enormous.

New connections

The Westerner, through only using the left side of his brain, does not use his capacity to think to its fullest. Use of both sides of the brain is necessary for that. The problem in the West is that the connection between the two halves of the brain doesn't function to its optimum. Also, in general, there is a distinction between men and women. Women have a 23% bigger connection between the two halves of their brain than men.

Brains can grow, according to new scientific research done in 1998. Not only can new connections be formed but also the brain cells can renew themselves. Before 1998, that wasn't yet proven in the West so it was considered 'not possible'.

Also, American research has shown that an external signal entering the body for the first time is initially registered in the area around the heart. Only then is the signal sent through to the brain.

It is possible to reactivate the connection between the two halves of the brain and to allow new connections to be formed. More connections mean a broader horizon and a deeper awareness. Through this you will live more in the here and now. The result of this is an exponential increase in the quality of your life because life is only available in the here and now. Your perception also increases with the growth in the number of connections and you can feel things (more deeply). Through this you are going to work more effectively and you will get more pleasure from your work.

Training

Training helps to reactivate the connection between the two halves of the brain. We don't have to worry too much about training the left side of our brain. We don't need to learn how to think in the way that we have already learned how to think. Also, the use of the right side doesn't have to give us too much concern. The hard part here is that we have to learn to go against our conditioning. Westerners' reasoning is mainly driven by fear. We are continuously busy with things that happened in the past or things that we want to or have to do in the future. Through this we are not focussed on the here and now, the only moment when we really can do things and perform. Living mindfully, as we call it, is anything but vague, as sceptics claim. Life is only available at this present moment in time. If we don't live in the here and now, we will be constantly hovering. Mindfulness is nothing more than being in the 'here and now'. That is all.

Mindfulness is becoming increasingly popular in psychotherapy because the results are so satisfying. There is also increasingly more fundamental research being done into mindfulness. Using these research results, such as the ones from an EEG, we can get an insight into what mindfulness does. You can measure brain frequency and concentration before and after a training session and find out how the person tested feels. From American research it has been shown that if you use and train mindfulness in the right way, within two weeks the participants will see substantial changes, both physically and mentally.

The right side of the brain is stimulated in a way that is contrary to that of the left side. We stuff the left side of our brain with all sorts of facts and figures; we activate the right side by 'emptying our head' of thoughts that have always been there. Many of us know the feeling of having a clear head when doing some intensive sport or when we are concentrating hard on a hobby.

You see quick results with mindfulness. Here's an example. Two teams have to get across an obstacle course as quickly as possible for a television programme. Which team can be the quickest? One team is led by a Sergeant Major – complete with moustache – the other one by a teacher of mindfulness. The mindfulness team will win.

More attention should be given in western training sessions to the wisdom of the body (as well as to the intelligence of the brain), the fact that we can learn more effectively by exerting ourselves physically. We should also pay more attention to the fact that working from intrinsic motivation has to be foremost. Westerners can learn to listen to their feelings with the help of mindfulness. People who start to live mindfully, begin to feel and experience things and they can recognise the early symptoms of stress. It's only once we become aware, that there is then room for change and innovation.

True quiet means keeping still when the time has come to keep still, and going forward when the time has come to go forward. In this way rest and movement are in agreement with the demands of the time.
- I-Ching, hexagram no. 52: Keeping still / Mountain

This chapter teaches us wise lessons that are similar to what we can learn thanks to iaido; they can be adapted to any situation, any moment and any place.

An old and a young monk are travelling through the country. The old monk has been a member of a strict Order for more than fifty years. The young monk has just joined. It is a great honour to be accepted into this Order but it does have very strong rules: the monks in this Order are not allowed to touch, look at or even talk to women.

One day the two monks come across a rickety old rope bridge. An old lady is standing in front of the bridge with a huge bundle of twigs on her back. Not knowing the Order of these monks, she asks them if they would help her get to the other side of the bridge.

The old monk walks up to her, picks her up, puts her onto his back, walks to the other side, puts the old lady down and continues along his way.

The young man has followed the whole escapade in a state of shock: the old monk will be cast out of the Order for what he's done! Totally confused and with tears in his eyes, he follows the old monk.

Three days later, having not dared to say a word to his leader, the young monk finally dares to say something and asks the old monk:

"Oh, old monk, how could you touch that old lady? Don't you realize that you could be thrown out of the Order?"

The old monk looks at him and says: "Yes, I did pick that old lady up, carried her and set her back down on the other side. You, on the other hand, my young friend, you've carried her around with you for three days already."

Basic rules for emptying your head

There are four simple basic rules for emptying your head:

Count the number times you breathe in and out

This is how you connect with the here and now. That's because you always breathe in the here and now. And then you can release your thoughts. Release, here, means: really let go. Very quickly, after just a few exercises, far less thoughts will come into your head. If you keep on practicing, the number of thoughts that come into your head will further decrease. Five minutes practice per day is enough. The only difficulty is in the repetition. You have to practice regularly. If necessary, you could choose a set time for it that will fit in with your personal circumstances.

Make sure your body is well balanced

A body that's in balance ensures that your mind is in balance. And this works the other way around too. Physical balance is easy to achieve by keeping both feet on the ground. Always keep both of your feet on the ground, even when you're sitting at your desk.

Relax
Stress is a phenomenon from the left side of our brain that obscures our view when overworked.

Be aware of your conditioning and fears
We are very good at continuously thinking about things that aren't there and that probably will never happen either. In most cases these thoughts are not functional and hold you back from achieving your goal.

These basic rules help you to use your own strength to find the right answer to the questions in this ever changing world, in any situation.
They help you to function with more pleasure and less stress and strain, and they lead to inner peace with a good perception. You don't have to work harder to achieve success, you can just relax.

It goes without saying that these four basic rules (breathing, balance, relaxation, and being aware) are linked and influence each another. They can be compared to communicating vessels. The more in balance you are, the better you can accommodate a lack of relaxation. Breathing, balance, relaxation and being aware get us ready to work using our own life force - instead of using force– and that is something that we also practice in iaido. Working with force costs energy, gathers resistance and demands a new supply of energy. Working from your own life force actually costs no energy and gathers no resistance. This improves our efficiency.

Imagine your perception as a mirror reflecting a pond full of fish. The wind is blowing hard. The surface of the pond is full of ripples created by the wind and it is impossible to see if there are any fish in the pond, let alone to see which way they are swimming.

Should one jump out of the water, it would make you jump. If left and right sides of the brain are connected and you live in the here and now, there is no more wind. Your head is peaceful and balanced. Through using the right side of your brain you are quicker than your conditioning; the surface of the water is as calm as crystal. Now you can see all the fish swimming in the pond and you can see the direction they are swimming in. A jumping fish would no longer make you jump.

Open up the thinking potential of our managers

Exercises from the Japanese art of Samurai swordsmanship help to open up the unused thinking potential of managers. Iaido puts you in a position so that you are able to activate the subconscious level, to consciously use it and to learn how to listen to it. The speed of thought at the subconscious level is ten times that at the conscious level.

Movement helps us to absorb information and turn it into knowledge. In the art of swordsmanship we couple the theory with movements, through which the knowledge enters us in a better way. When we move we bring our brain into the alpha state of mind. We achieve the alpha state of mind when our brain frequency is between 7 and 14 hertz. At that moment 'the gateway' to the subconscious is open and that is the optimal way of learning. This has also been proven in various pieces of research. For example, people who lie on the sofa in an alpha state of mind and listen to a language course, can learn a language in just six weeks.

Tips for managers on how to make contact with their employees

Know your people!
Make contracts for personal development, instead of a job description.
Delegate tasks, such as marketing and responsibility for personnel.

Delegate tasks, such as marketing and responsibility for personnel.
When giving rewards, the emphasis should be on how independently the employee works and the quality of the work (so, not on production!).
Offer work experience opportunities in other departments - change cranks up creativity.
Split your people up into two groups and give each group a manager. These managers keep note of what their own group is doing and what the other group does. If one group does better, the other can learn from them.
Walk through the company (and get your posture right!)

Rewarding change

Of course companies want to achieve better results year on year. And they are reliant on their staff for this. The leaders that try to get the most out of their staff, often do this in the wrong way. 80% of the time they will encourage their people by talking them into doing something. And according to Mathieu Weggeman, Professor of Organisational Science, specialising in Innovation Management at the Faculty of Technical Management at Eindhoven University, that doesn't work well.
Behavioural change can be brought about by using old fashioned conditioning principles such as punishing undesirable behaviour and rewarding the desired behaviour. But from the 20% of their time that leaders use for behavioural change, some 80% is put into punishing undesirable behaviour. Whilst punishment makes sure that employees take not one extra step further. Punishment leads to a compliance culture based on fear, Weggeman suggests. And that clashes with innovation and creativity. In the long term, this way of working is counter-productive. People only learn what is not allowed, and don't find out what the proper intention is. It has become so popular because with punishment or by threatening, you see direct results.

Leaders don't consciously choose for this kind of approach. Often they act out of fear or they have a lack of knowledge. You see this especially in employees that have been promoted from a specialist position to a leadership position. Plenty of research has shown that rewarding positive behaviour delivers more. Don't reward with money, but with compliments, a staff outing or a piece of cake during the coffee break. The strength of this kind of reward is that it is directly followed by good behaviour. Employees feel more open through it. So if leaders say that it isn't possible to change their staff, it's just that they don't know how they should handle them.
The sword doesn't change. So you have to adapt to the sword. You can't change your surroundings. They only change once you have changed.

The advantage of a positive impulse is that employees are then willing to take that little extra step. Compliments work as a stimulant for all employees. The right reward can differ from staff member to staff member. One will like extra days off, another would prefer a book or some music. According to Weggeman, it is very important that leaders clearly describe which results and which behaviour he is wanting to change. And the leader also has to change. He can no longer enforce change through using punishment, but he has to look at what is going well, who is performing well and how he can reward that. Not with bonuses, but with compliments and attention.

Apply the basic rules

When you apply the basic rules, you get inner peace and an oversight of the whole situation. Thoughts no longer bounce around in your head but they can, at any moment, be focussed on one particular task. Through this, it is possible to anticipate what is going to happen in this changing world, without just taking the safe path that others have travelled before you.

This is where the crux of creativity and efficiency lies. Efficiency isn't the same as doing lots of things at the same time so that you are finished more quickly. It is only when you no longer do unnecessary things that you will be finished more quickly. But why the rush?

Creativity is much more important and for the most part it is linked to your intrinsic motivation. Everyone already has their own natural motivation. Really, having to motivate someone shouldn't be necessary. You can teach someone how to see where their intrinsic motivation is by showing where their need to 'feel good' comes from.

You are doing enough just by applying the four basic rules, but that seems easier than it really is. The crux is that you have to be consistent in continuing to apply the basic rules. We know how you should do a lot of things but you have to make an effort to keep them up. It really is much easier if you just keep doing them, no matter how hard and difficult it may appear from the outside. Once you know how to apply one or more of the basic rules, you will feel better and stronger, immediately.

The pupils at the Muso Shinden Ryu (one of the oldest iaido schools) use the four rules to practice the many forms of fighting with imaginary opponents. Using the basic rules you can simulate many, often seemingly complicated, forms of fighting. You can take on the whole spectrum of possibilities and experiences from a period of three whole centuries on the Japanese battle field. In principal, therefore, the four basic rules give you the capability to be able to give the right answer in any situation, on your own.

The basic rules bring the connection between the two halves of the brain into action. You use the information that is registered in your sub consciousness much better. Awareness follows unawareness, usually without our even realising. We Westerners notice that too.

We often sleep on something for a night before we make a decision. We don't buy a car if we don't have a good gut feeling about it. As Ab Dijksterhuis suggests: our subconscious (or unconscious mind) has decided something, so later our conscious mind thinks up a suitable explanation for this.

One day, Albert, a sixteen year old boy, was lying on his back in the grass, sometime around 1895, and he was looking at how the sunbeams shining through the leaves of the trees formed stripes on the ground. He tried to work out how he could sit on one of those sunbeams and fly along the earth. He wondered what he would see. Ten years later he published an article about his dream, that we now know as the Theory of Relativity.
Einstein didn't know a lot about physics and failed his university entrance exam. He daydreamed a lot and worked using his intuition, the right side of his brain. That is where he thought or dreamed up his theories, which he later worked out with the left side of his brain.

The subconscious is so much bigger than our consciousness or awareness. You can compare it to an iceberg with its tip showing abovethe water. The tip (some 15%) is the awareness, the subconscious (some 85%) is under the surface of the water. Our subconscious contains more than just the information that we store in there during our lifetime. The storage capacity of our subconscious is much bigger than that of our conscious mind. The conscious mind thinks that it knows how to do something, the subconscious knows how to do it. Thanks to awareness, you learn how to look at things as they really are. You let go of the things that you have always thought and you transform knowledge into insight. Knowledge hangs around permanently and we can switch from one (problem) area to the other much faster. If we learn how to trust our intuition, we are much better prepared to apply our acquired knowledge in many more situations.

When explaining the art of studying, learning, the taking possession of knowledge and skills, the I-Ching puts the emphasis on repetition, in any kind of situation.

Water gives the example as to how one should behave in such circumstances. It is continually flowing and simply fills up every nook and cranny that it flows past. It doesn't shrink from anything – not from a dangerous spot, not from a steep drop into the deep – and it never loses its essential character. [...] Once one becomes master of the situation internally, then everything will just happen naturally and the things one does externally will bring success. [...] Water achieves its goal by flowing on uninterruptedly. It fills up every abyss before flowing on. [...] Also when teaching others, it is all about being consistent. It is only through repetition that the pupil will absorb the knowledge.

- I CHING, HEXAGRAM NO. 29 – THE ABYSMAL / WATER

Epilogue

Through this book I hope to be able to provide some contribution towards a healthier business world that combines the wisdom of the East with that of the West. This book shouldn't be seen as a reading book that once read through can be just put back on the bookshelf, never to see the light of day again. If we in the West really want to take a big step towards an economy that can serve its employees, customers and society, then we will have to become more open to other ideas. The well known saying 'you can't solve a problem with the same mind that created it' is often quoted – you then usually see lots of nodding heads, agreeing with it – and we follow this up by just getting on with the order of the day. Business as usual.

The problems that the western business world and the western population currently have to deal with are so exhaustive that 'just carrying on in the same way' is no longer an option. We either have to change our way of looking at life and at ourselves, fundamentally, or we will go under. There is no halfway. Each past civilization was brought down in the end by self-satisfaction, egotism and the inability to change or adapt to changing circumstances. I have every hope that our civilization will wake up in time. The most important ingredient needed to wake us up is the awareness that our civilization has crashed into the end of a dead end street, regardless of the profit we have made over the last few decades. That awareness is growing.

Increasingly, for the younger generation, CSR or Corporate Social Responsibility is not seen as an option for possibly earning yet more money, but it is the natural choice. The interest in spirituality is increasing enormously in the West. Apparently, there is a great need to find another way. Every book or idea can help with this but at the end of the day it all boils down to ourselves.

Only if we can accept full, one hundred percent, responsibility for everything that happens in our life, can actual steps be taken. Becoming aware and changing is an inner process. Everything begins and ends here. My experience has shown me that the Way of the Sword is a fitting and pleasurable way that strengthens and speeds up this process.

About Bjørn Aris

Even as a young boy, I liked to test my boundaries. Not only physically, but also within myself.

Once, when I was just seven years old, I really wanted to play outside but the teacher wouldn't allow it. After a couple of attempts at sneaking out of the classroom, the teacher promised that if I did a long division calculation, then I could go and play outside.

When I'd handed in my long division, I waited for the teacher to tell me that I could go outside but instead she said that I had to do another sum. But that wasn't the deal. As I had twice tried to run outside, the classroom door was locked. So I jumped out of the window. And we were one storey up! Because I'd been taking judo lessons for a number of years already, I landed neatly on my feet, did a quick forward roll and off I went.

Not long after that I went to another school. Looking back I suppose that there was maybe a causal connection here ...

Secondary school was really interesting due to all the extracurricular activities. Once I'd got my VWO diploma (the Dutch equivalent of 'A levels' or High School graduation), I was registered as a law student for a while, after which I went into the military service with the SROKI – the School Reserve Officers and Infantry Management– in Ermelo.

Towards the end of my secondary school education, I started training at the distinguished jiu-jitsu school run by Bob van Nieuwenhuizen, one of the instigators of jiu-jitsu in The Netherlands. Years later I would become a teacher at that same school, something I never dreamed could be possible at that time.

I had a lot of fun in the military service and learned two important things. The first was: respect for everyone, and the second: that the spirit is stronger than the body. Even under abominable circumstances (temperatures of -28C) the body can keep going, if you have the right focus.

After the military service I started working for Amro Bank, as a Commercial Officer. They almost didn't take me on because when they asked me how I saw my future career – something I had never thought about, in fact something I still haven't thought about – I answered: as a Board Member. Why have boundaries?

Seven years, five internal jobs (all going up the job scales) and a whole range of bank training courses later, I was invited by Lloyds Bank to continue my career with them. In the meantime, for the last ten years and three times a week, I was to be found training on the jiu-jitsu mat. Alongside this, I had developed an increasingly broader interest in Japan, Samurai and Zen.

Whilst at Lloyds I learned about International Banking and within two years I was heading up their Corporate Finance team.

More and more, I was living in two worlds and slowly but surely my daytime world (banking and clientele) was beginning to split itself off from my evening and weekend world of the Samurai and Zen.

During my first Zen session, I was sitting on a cushion in a suit. I noticed that the people around me not only looked very different to me but they were also talking about notions that were totally unknown to me. I decided to buy a book about Zen. I read it through and didn't understand a word. So, back to the bookshop and I bought another book. Once I'd read this one, it was still totally unclear to me what it was all about. But, keep on trying ... so a third book was purchased. This was also incomprehensible. In the meantime, three months had passed during which I'd been visiting my Zen teacher every week and was also training daily at home. Instead of buying a fourth book, I decided to pick up the first one again. And all of a sudden ... I understood what it was about. Brilliant! Training seems to change your brain, through which your horizon broadens, your awareness gets deeper and your understanding gets bigger.

When I was 32 years old, I did the first commercial securitisation for Lloyds and I already had the feeling of 'what am I doing here?' You tie a legally and fiscally technical ribbon around a piece of your balance sheet, shove a bit of it onto paper, stick a rubber stamp on it (at the Rating Agencies') and hey presto! ... all of a sudden there is money available in America for a traditional Dutch company with no international connections. Whilst in reality, nothing has changed.

It was time to change course. I resigned, sold my house, left my girlfriend and set off, with just a rucksack on my back, to travel around Africa, the Middle East, Asia, Oceania and Japan.

The first part in Africa was difficult. I had never been a Boy Scout and was used to a luxury Corporate Banker's lifestyle; and there I was, all of a sudden with the task of making a fire in the middle of the bush, and it just wouldn't light. After just three weeks I'd been attacked by an elephant, an eagle had tried to dive bomb me, I was nearly trodden to death by a hippo whilst sleeping in my pathetic little tent and all sorts of smaller creatures, including some rather nasty specimens, had taken a fancy to me and bitten me half way to death.

This was so stressful that I just thought: "oh well, you know what, if I die right now, then so be it." And at that moment it was as if an enormous weight had been lifted from my shoulders. All of a sudden I was ready to leave my head and enter my body, through which I felt connected to my surroundings and I could to listen to my own intuition.

This kind of feeling happened to me twice in those first three months in Africa. The rest of the trip, that took me far from the beaten track, went very harmoniously, just by following my intuition. There were plenty of thrilling moments, that's for sure, but they just added colour to the whole picture.

Although I had no real reason to return to the Netherlands, I decided to do it anyway, especially as, at that time (1998) the Netherlands was the richest country in the World. It was one of the few countries in the World where you could find six different kinds of mustard, side by side on the shelf in the supermarket and even more importantly, here you were free to say whatever you wanted to – with the only risk being that people may look at you a little sympathetically.

During those first few months back in the Netherlands, I noticed how people were always in a hurry and how they worried about all sorts of small things that might never happen. I couldn't understand it. In order to earn a bit of money, I went back to the banking world. After a short period back at Lloyds, I was invited to go and work for another bank, NIB (now NIBC).

What I especially noticed in that period of my life was that a lot of things happened without a clear reason. Coming up with a solution to a problem within ten minutes, based purely on intuition, wasn't considered acceptable. No, first you had to think about it for a long time, work really hard at it, write pages full of words – and only then could you come up with the right solution. After the English way of thinking I'd seen at Lloyds, I was now faced with the Calvinistic way of thinking at NIB.

At the end of 1999, a friend called me with the question: "Shall we do something together in this internet hype?" "Brilliant," I replied, "because I know absolutely nothing about that." You couldn't wish for a better start.

After all, if you know nothing, you can look at things with an open mind, and if you think that it is possible, then it is possible. On the other hand, if you look at things 'from experience', you quickly see wolves hiding behind the trees and obstacles in your path and you think: now, I don't know if this will work. And – what a surprise – you were right, it doesn't work.

The business was a success and just before the market went down, I decided to sell my half of the shares.

Yet I still felt that something wasn't right with the life that I was leading. Of course, it was great, a successful upward moving career in the corporate banking world; it was great, setting up and selling a successful business ... But it was time to get serious. And that means: concentrating on what is inside of you. Because happiness can't be found on the outside, in a material form, it's on the inside, in the form of experience.

I started studying intuitive development, healing, reading and light working. I then qualified in neurofeedback, I did a course on physiological studies about the human body and the four levels of consciousness as we see them in the West, I practiced jiu-jitsu, iaido and zen and studied Eastern philosophy. By this stage, I had been training Eastern martial arts for more than 20 years, five days a week. I was also giving a few hours of lessons per week in iaido in my own dojo.

In 2004 I wrote a paper for the Knowledge Management State of the Art Congress. In this paper I proposed that model thinking and superficial intellectualism don't work, but investment in people, knowledge and learning, do.

The paper was picked out from the many submissions that were made and was chosen to be included in the book *Het effect van investeren in mensen, kennis en leren (The Effect of Investing in People, Knowledge and Learning).*

On the back of this I started giving interactive lectures about and training courses in personal effectiveness and leadership to people in middle and top management, from Nairobi to Amersfoort.

In 2007, at the request of Kluwer (a large Dutch international organisation) and as a result of some articles I'd written for *Het Financiele Dagblad (the Dutch equivalent of the Financial Times),* I developed a Kluwer Management Tool. In 'Effectief management op basis van oosterse principes' (Effective management based on Eastern principles), I explain the differences between a manager and a leader and what we can learn from the East in order to solve recurring western problems.

I now give training courses to many (large) companies in Europe and further afield. From research, (based on answers given by employees from Air France-KLM, Nijenrode University and Logica who participated in my training sessions), my training sessions appear to be highly valued thanks to the interactive element, amongst other things. Two to six months after the training course, 70% of the participants could still reproduce the essence of the training course, and 83% of the participants had actually started actively using what they had learned.

I am the very proud father of Magnus and Freja and I live in a house near the beach in Scheveningen.

Acknowledgements

I owe many thanks to all of the people in my life. For meeting me, the resonance, the pleasure, the lessons, the love, the fights, the smiles, the tears, the help ... for being there and for not being there.

The following teachers have played a great role in my evolvement as a Japanese swordsman: Bob and Steve van Nieuwenhuizen sensei, Gerard Stijf sensei, Makoto Kurabe sensei, Ishido Shizufumi sensei and Aad van de Wijngaart sensei.

I am especially grateful to my teacher Javier Velazquez. He is a true bodhisattva. I consider it a great privilege to have had lessons from him, covering so much ground.

Thanks to Willem Vreeswijk sensei who has helped me so much with the putting together of this book – from the beginning to the very end.

Sources

I Ching (ed. R. Wilhelm).
B. Aris, 'Effectief management op basis van oosterse principes'. (Article in Kluwer database)
F. Goodman, website.
J.K. Liker, *The Toyota Way, 14 Management Principles from the World's Greatest Manufacturer.*
D. Lowry, *Sword and Brush: The Spirit of Martial Arts.*
D. Lowry, *In the Dojo.*
D. Lowry, *Moving Toward Stillness.*
P. Reps, *Zen-zin Zen-onzin.*
D. Russell, *Kuniyasu Sakai en Hiroshi Sekiyama As Told to David Russell.*
R. Shea, *Shike: Last of the Zinja.*
C. Stam (et al.), *Kennisproductiviteit. Het effect van investeren in mensen, kennis en leren.*
S. Tsutyoshi Ohnishi (et al.), *Philosophy, Psychology, Physics and Practice of Ki.* (Paper from the Dept. of Biochemistry and Biophysics, University of Pennsylvania School of Medicine.)
P. West, *IAIDO Handbook BKA (British Kendo Organisation),* 1995.
Articles from www.returnonpeople.nl
Articles from www.wikipedia.com

Notes to the Text

1 See also: D. Russell, *Kuniyasu Sakai en Hiroshi Sekiyama As Told to David Russell.*

2 J. Vuist, in a magazine column, but unfortunately I can't remember which magazine it was or the date it appeared.

3 From Frans Johansson, *Medici Effect.*

4 Adaptation of text in S. Tsutyoshi Ohnishi (et al.), *Philosophy, Psychology, Physics and Practice of Ki.*

5 Adaptation of text by Fay Goodman, from her website some years ago.

6 Quote from R. Shea, *Shike: Last of the Zinja.*

7 Adaptation of text in D. Lowry, *Sword and Brush.*

7 Adaptation of text on Wikipedia.

9 Adaptation of a piece of text in D. Lowry, *Sword and Brush.*

10 Quote from D. Lowry, *In the Dojo.*

11 Quote from D. Lowry, *In the Dojo.*

12 Quote from Haruna Matsua Nanadan Kyoshi, from the IAIDO Handbook BKA.

13 Adaptation of a piece of text in D. Lowry, *Moving Toward Stillness.*

14 Matsuoku and Kinomoto sensei, as heard by the author.

15 Adaptation of a piece of text in D. Lowry, *Sword and Brush.*

16 Free adaptation of Paul Reps, *Zen-zin Zen-onzin.*

17 Quote from the IAIDO Handbook BKA.

Author's Media

RETURN ON
PEOPLE

www.returnonpeople.nl

THE CUTTING EDGE

The Martial Art of Business

www.bjornaris.com

The power of the sword | TEDxDordrecht |
Video

Outside in. A way to freedom
Video

"We say, to shine one corner of the World – that is enough.

Not the whole World. Just make it clear where you are."

SHUNRYU SUZUKI